Docherty

Brian Clarke is an experienced
member of the Piccadilly
Radio sports team in
Manchester, commentating
mainly on soccer. He is the
author of the highly successful
Murphy's Law, the authorised
biography of Rugby League's
Alex Murphy.

BRIAN CLARKE

Docherty

a biography of Tommy Docherty

Mandarin

A Mandarin Paperback
DOCHERTY

First published in Great Britain 1991
by The Kingswood Press
This edition published 1992
by Mandarin Paperbacks
Michelin House, 81 Fulham Road, London SW3 6RB

Mandarin is an imprint of Reed Consumer Books Ltd

Copyright © 1991 Brian Clarke
The author has asserted his moral rights

A CIP catalogue record for this title
is available from the British Library
ISBN 0 7493 0730 7

Printed and bound in Great Britain
by Cox & Wyman Ltd, Cardiff Road, Reading

Contents

Acknowledgements   vii
1 The Boy from Nowhere   1
2 Deepdale Days   7
3 A Hero at Highbury   33
4 Chelsea: Crossing the Bridge   44
5 Rocked at Blackpool   61
6 Europe, and Double Trouble   74
7 Brighton and Bermuda   100
8 On the Move   111
9 Shaking Up Old Trafford   124
10 Past his Best   146
11 Resign, or Else . . .   153
12 In the Courts   169
13 Docherty Speaking   182

Acknowledgements

The writing of this book would not have been possible without the special help given me by Michael Page, and by David Barber of the Football Association, Kelly Cockerell of Chelsea Football Club, Kate Grimwade, Alan Pinnock, Tony Pocock, Neil Tunnicliffe and Westminster Central Reference Library, to all of whom my thanks are due.

I am especially grateful to the sports editor of *The Times* for his generosity in allowing me to quote from the reports of nine matches, by various writers including Norman Fox, Tom Freeman and Geoffrey Green, in which Tommy Docherty took part as player or as manager; and similar thanks are due to John Donald Publishers, of Edinburgh, for allowing me to quote from James Leatherdale's book *Scotland's Quest for the World Cup*.

The photographs have been reproduced by kind permission of Associated Newspapers (Nos. 7, 16), Associated Press (No. 10), Barratt's Photo Press (No. 6), R. Broome (No. 27), Central Press (No. 3), Colorsport (Nos. 21, 22, 23, 25, 26), Daily Mail (No. 11), Daily Mirror Newspapers (No. 13), Evening Standard (No. 18), George Outram (No. 4), Planet News (No. 1), Press Association (Nos. 8, 14), Thomson Newspapers (No. 9) and John Varley (No. 24).

Brian Clarke

1 The Boy from Nowhere

Tommy Docherty needed no cause to be a rebel. Born into the toughness and hardships of one of Glasgow's poorest districts between the wars, he never lost the combative spirit that as player, manager and, indeed, man made him one of his country's most famous, and famously controversial, sportsmen. If you wanted results, you sent for Docherty; but often there was a price to pay.

As a player of world class he achieved the rare distinction of not only captaining his country's national side, but later managing them as well. As a manager in the Football League he forged teams for which the only description is that soccer cliché 'magic', forged them moreover out of some very thin steel indeed. But all the time there was an impulsive streak, almost it seemed a self-destruct button, that impelled him into controversy, that led him from the heights to the depths not just once, but twice. Outspoken, often outrageous, he was unyielding if his authority was challenged (whether by teenage apprentice or by chairman) and the rules – his rules – were broken.

A tough man. Yet when Manchester United lost their relegation battle during his first season with them he unashamedly shed tears in front of reporters, and he was capable of generating great fun for everyone around him. He had a deep loyalty towards his players, fighting their cause even if dressing-room rebellion was in the air. And there lies the basic and most interesting paradox. For here was a man who could take a group of raw youngsters and coax, bludgeon, blend, motivate them into being men with the soccer world at their feet with all the fame and the financial rewards so implied . . . and yet many of those same young men rebelled against him, when one would have expected them to follow him through hell-fire itself. It happened at Stamford Bridge, and discontent followed him to Old Trafford.

Of course, not everyone was his detractor. Life is not so black-and-white. There are many, players and management, who will tell you he was brushed with genius (which in all fairness is hard to dispute) but that he was a victim of circumstances, of jealousy and various other hazards of life. Certainly the media loved him; he was always ready with a good, punchy, often funny quote on every aspect of the game from hooliganism to the relative merits of Best and Pelé. It is a matter of personal standpoint.

Of one thing we can be certain, however: no one could be, nor can be, indifferent to 'the Doc'. Perhaps the definitive epitaph comes from one of his Manchester United stars, Steve Coppell: 'Managers are not made in heaven.'

In what most men would regard as hard-earned retirement, Docherty is now as active as ever on the after-dinner circuit, machine-gunning his famous one-liners to the delight of his audiences. He lives comfortably in Derbyshire, fast-talking, quick-moving, strangely reminiscent of James Cagney, greeting visitors with the approach of a man going into a tackle. And even now he refuses to conform. Proud Scotsman though he is, he prefers champagne to whisky and his only empathy with golf is to watch it occasionally on television.

Thomas Henderson Docherty was born on 24 April 1928 into the harsh realities of a Glasgow tenement slum and was christened at St Anne's Roman Catholic church. Poverty and hardship went virtually unremarked in the daily fight for survival in the infamous Gorbals district, where childhood illnesses were a constant threat to family life already under attack from the overcrowded, Dickensian conditions. The Dochertys – father Thomas, mother Georgina, Tommy, and younger sister Margaret – lived in a cramped single room and slept on bed boards that jutted from the walls. There was a wash basin in the room, but the outside toilet was shared with a number of families. Friday night was the highlight of the week, when the children would be scrubbed clean in the big tin bath before the fire.

It was a hard and hostile environment, but Docherty looks back on it with warmth and affection. Despite everything the family was always well fed and very well looked after, and was a happy unit. There was a shadow over them, however, for their father was battling against ill health. He worked as a labourer at Stuart and Lloyd, a local iron foundry, and was to die shortly before Tommy's ninth birthday.

Before then, though, a slight improvement came in their living conditions when they moved to a house in Gallowgate, but even there Mrs Docherty had to take turns with a neighbour to clean the shared outdoor toilet. Then came luxury: a house with not only an inside toilet but with a sitting-room, two smaller rooms and its own kitchen, too. For the first time young Tommy was experiencing a style of life that nowadays is regarded as the minimum, and as he says now, it was like living in the south of France.

About that time, Docherty the footballer began to emerge. At his new school, St Mark's in Shettleston, he played as often as he could and trained whenever he couldn't. Even so early he was a fitness fanatic, an aspect of the game that would be carried not only into his professional playing days but also into his time in management; a Docherty team was always an outstandingly fit team.

On Saturday mornings he would play centre-half for his school team, then dash home for a bite to eat before turning out in the afternoon for a youth side run by the local priest, Fr Joseph Connolly, a regular visitor to the Docherty home who always encouraged his football. Tommy's ambition was to play for Glasgow Celtic, and by great good fortune the family now lived near Celtic's ground at Parkhead. On match days the gates would be opened twenty minutes before the end of the game to let the supporters leave early for their buses home, so Tommy could then slip into the ground for nothing. Even so there was always the friendly gateman who would be willing to lift youngsters over the turnstile to watch the last few minutes without paying. It meant that Tommy was able to watch a lot of top-class football that otherwise he could never have been able to afford. The game was his life even then. His school teacher used to tell him, 'Frankly, Docherty, football's all you're fit for.' Academically, he didn't seem to be rated. Certainly he played for anyone who offered him a game and regularly for the St Paul's Guild team.

His schooling was finished at 14, and it was time to help with the family's upkeep. His first job was at the local pottery on wages of 25s 9d (about £1.35) a week, a small fortune to the boy used to second-hand clothes and handouts. His widowed mother, working as a charwoman to provide for her children, gave his first week's wages to the Church by way of saying thank you to Fr Connolly for the support he had given the family over the years. The harsh realities of working life came home forcibly to the young Docherty in only his second week at the pottery when a strike was called and everyone was sacked. Undaunted, he went to the local bakery but the routine of starting in the early hours was a punishing one and he packed the job in after his second day.

A job as a window cleaner seemed promising, for he fancied the idea of an outdoor working life, but after three days he found he was allergic to heights. His next try, as a factory labourer, made him hope for a little more permanence. His wish was granted: a full week passed before conditions began to irritate his skin and he threw the towel in. Knowing that his mother relied on his small income, he was off again on the job trail, this time to Shettleston Bottle Works. Long hours and shift work interrupted his football and his training schedules, however, and he walked out after three weeks. Then came the job that suited him: as a van boy delivering bread. The hours allowed him to train and play football.

By now – just before the Second World War – football scouts were beginning to take notice of the fit, strong-running forward. He got his first offer, from the local non-league side Shettleston Juniors: £3 signing-on fee plus expenses. If the team played well they had a share of the gate money.

Even when he was called up into the army with the Highland Light Infantry in 1946 Docherty continued to play for his local team, thanks to weekend passes. His name was spreading, and Newcastle United and Burnley both invited him for trials, but he had only one burning ambition . . . to play for Glasgow Celtic, 'the biggest club in Britain'.

2 Deepdale Days

Strangely, it was a posting to Palestine that moved Docherty towards a career in professional football. For his first big representative match he was chosen for the British Army team alongside others destined for top-class football, players such as Adam Little of Rangers and Arthur Rowley, brother of the future England centre-forward Jack, who made his name with Manchester United. Another was Lt. Walter Waddell, the brother of Willie, the famous Scottish international winger: 'I think he probably put a word in for me and my name was known when I returned home.'

Home from the Middle East for demob in July 1948, Docherty still had no firm plans for a career. But someone – possibly some of his Army team-mates – had been spreading the word, and several leading clubs showed an interest. In fact he actually arrived home (carrying his demob suit because he had 'looked ridiculous' when he tried it on at the York demob centre) to find three managers waiting to talk to him. Two of them were Stan Seymour from Newcastle United and Cliff Britton from Burnley. The third was Jimmy McCrory from Celtic. The result was a foregone conclusion. As Docherty puts it now,

The next day I was at Parkhead signing. Celtic offered
me £9 a week during the season and £7 a week in the
summer. After army pay that put me in the millionaire
class, but I was so keen to play for them I would
have gone for nothing. I couldn't believe my luck. My
mother was pleased too. She was a staunch Catholic
and loved Celtic. Religious loyalties were very strong.

It may have been a dream come true, but it was to
be shortlived and disillusionment soon overtook him.
Despite reports from the coaching staff that he would
one day play for Scotland as a wing-half, he could not
hold down a first-team place. The man who kept him out
was Bobby Evans, a regular in the Scottish team. If Evans
was playing for Scotland or was injured then Docherty got
his chance, but mostly the newcomer was playing in the
reserves, and as he admits, 'I was too ambitious for that.'
It was a double frustration for Docherty, who felt that if
he had been a couple of inches over his 5ft 8in he would
have been the outstanding centre-half in Scotland.

The dilemma was to solve itself. After little more than
a year Docherty was called into the office by manager
Jimmy McCrory, who asked him if he would like to try
his luck in English football. It was a blow. Celtic, the club
of his boyhood dreams, did not want him. The possibility
of a move south of the border became more attractive,
however, when it was pointed out that Preston North
End, one of the leading teams in England at that time,
were willing to pay him £10 a week even in the summer
and were also offering him a club house. It was too good
an opportunity to miss. Celtic quickly restored his faith

by giving him a £750 golden goodbye to help with the cost of moving south.

It also helped him set up house, for while he was with Celtic he had met a girl named Agnes. On 27 December 1949, just a few weeks after arriving in Preston, he was back in Scotland to marry her in her home town of Girvan. They were to have a daughter and three sons, of whom Michael was to follow his father and become first a professional footballer with Burnley, Manchester City and Sunderland before going on to a management career with Sunderland.

Tommy Cavanagh, the reserve team inside-right who later would be Docherty's number two at Manchester United and his confidant in difficult times, recalls the impact he made when he arrived at Preston. Manager Will Scott had ordered Cavanagh to meet Docherty at the railway station when he arrived from Scotland: 'He stood out. He was wearing a green sports jacket and grey flannels and had floppy blond hair. There was an air of cockiness about him. I liked him straightaway. He asked me to take him to the nearest Catholic church. I think he wanted to say a prayer for his new career. It sticks in my mind, that moment. I was the first player he met and we struck up a bond together. We have been pals ever since. He was such a good passer of the ball. His passing was like Tom Finney's, inch-perfect. So often in a match Docherty would thread a perfect pass through to Finney and the master would do the rest. He was also a good leader on the field.'

Will Scott had paid £4,000 for Docherty and had no

doubts about his bargain: 'It's only a matter of time before this lad plays for his country,' he told the local newspaper. 'He thinks of football all the time and keeps himself in peak physical condition. He's a tremendous trainer.'

Cavanagh recognised why Docherty was such a fanatical trainer: 'He was a player who liked to go forward helping out in attack, but if it broke down and the opposition regained possession he had the energy to get back and defend. He could play flat out for the whole game.'

In the closing weeks of the 1949–50 season Docherty was named fifteen times in the Preston first team as he established himself as the regular right-half. In his second season – during which he was becoming a regular member of the Scottish reserve squad – he played in every match as the team won the second-division Championship and promotion. On the way Preston equalled a record set forty-five years earlier by Bristol City of fourteen consecutive League victories in the season. And the step up to the first division in August 1951 posed no problem for Docherty as he again played in every League game. His consistency was maintained, and in a match at Highbury in 1953 the Arsenal manager Tom Whittaker lavished praise on him for his display as Preston drew 1–1 with the title-chasing Londoners. Arsenal had managed to equalise only in the closing stages with a goal from Joe Mercer to keep their Championship hopes alive. Docherty's performance was described as 'peerless' by the press with most reports naming him as the man-of-the-match.

In all, Docherty notched up 323 games for Preston,

but the beginning of November 1949 is etched indelibly in Docherty's mind not only as the start of his career in English football, but also as the beginning of a lifelong friendship with Tom Finney, a man he sums up as simply the greatest all-round player he ever saw or played alongside.

> He had everything. He could measure a pass to the inch, had tremendous balance and ball control. He could head the ball as accurately as anyone I have ever seen and could shoot with either foot. Today you would have to sell a club to buy him. Besides all that, he was a gentleman on and off the field and an inspirational captain. If Tom was tackled unfairly you never heard him complain or retaliate. I became a much better player watching him and listening to him. His enthusiasm for the game never wavered. He had a genuine love for football.

Many years later, when asked if a certain highly rated young winger was as good as Finney, Docherty's answer was instant: 'Yes, but Tom's now in his 60s.'

Just before the start of the third round of the FA Cup in 1954 Docherty broke an ankle in a practice match, but such was his dedication and determination that he was back remarkably quickly and able to take his full part in a team by then playing what was probably the highest-quality football in the country. 'Brilliant' was the word often used about them, and nowhere else was it more justified than in their triumphant passage to the final against West Bromwich Albion.

Leicester City was the side that gave them the most

trouble en route to Wembley – and that was in the third round, at Filbert Street. Preston seemed safe, leading 1–0 in the closing minutes, but then a free-kick was lobbed over the defenders to force a replay. Preston, playing at home, foresaw no great problems, but found themselves 0–2 down and their Cup interests fading fast. Then Charlie Wayman, all 5ft 5in of him and the man Docherty names as the best footballing centre-forward of his time (but who was never capped for England), cracked in a goal, to be followed by Angus Morrison with another. In extra time both sides hit the post, so they went on to Hillsborough for another replay. This time, with some relief, Preston settled the debate with a 3–1 win. More typical of them was the semi-final at Maine Road, when the 2–0 margin over Sheffield Wednesday could have been a lot more; Finney was in great form as Preston spent most of the match in Wednesday's half of the pitch.

Their League performances can be summed up in an away game against Spurs shortly before the Cup final. Without Finney or Wayman, and playing four reserves, Preston still won 6–2, to inspire Ron Burgess the Spurs captain to ask them, 'Why don't you take the Cup back with you now, and save the train fare? The way you're playing, the final is a formality.'

It was, however, an anticlimax. What should have been the final of the decade, between two sides that between them blended most of the arts and sciences of the game, was a flop. Neither Preston nor West Bromwich played to their proven potential; but as Docherty has said, 'Of two poor performances, theirs was just a mite better.'

The crux for Preston was that Finney had an off-day, his genius shackled. Both teams took a little time feeling one another out before Cunningham, Preston's right-back, tried to find Finney; the ball hit WBA's Lee instead, Lee recovered it, ran on with it and shot. The ball seemed to be going yards wide when Ronnie Allen moved up and side-footed it into the net. It was that kind of a day for Preston. But they quickly got back when Docherty lobbed the ball to the far post for Morrison to head in.

Things seemed to be moving Preston's way as they began to show their true form, seven or eight men going forward in a characteristic series of first-time passes. Docherty slipped the ball through to Wayman, who put it into the net. Most of the players, however, knew he was a good twenty yards off-side . . . but the goal was allowed. Preston 2 WBA 1. Then, disaster. Counter-attacking vigorously, West Bromwich's left-half Ray Barlow overran the ball. Docherty slid into him as he was trying to regain control, Barlow was down, and the referee gave a penalty. Docherty maintains to this day that photos of the incident prove that he had taken the ball fairly – and also that an injured WBA player had come back on to the field during the move without the referee's permission and at the tackle was standing in an off-side position.

Literally in the last minute of ordinary time Albion broke away and Preston goalkeeper Thompson made one of the nightmare mistakes that are always likely to happen in the charged atmosphere of a final. If he had stayed where he was he would almost certainly have saved the shot; instead he dived at Griffin's feet, the ball was pushed gently under his body, hit the far post and rolled slowly into the net.

So the casually confident and aristocratic Preston side came off the Wembley pitch almost unnoticed, as is the fate of Cup losers. To a man, the side felt a deep sorrow for Tom Finney. He had carried Preston for years, and everyone had wanted a winner's medal for him to climax his career.

Analysing it later, Docherty thought the crucial error was in Preston's planning for the game. The manager broke routine and took the side to Weybridge near London almost a week before the final, when all through their run-up to the Cup they had trained at home and then left on the Friday. As it was, they did no training at all after the Wednesday before the big match. Hotel life does nothing to sharpen up an athlete at the best of times and the Preston side lived merely from one meal to the next, sitting around, growing more lethargic by the hour. With nothing else to concentrate on, Wembley loomed in their minds, and eager as they were for the match, tension set in. Every now and again someone would look at his watch and say, 'We'll know, this time on Saturday.'

On match day, they purposely arrived at the ground only an hour or so before kick-off, so that they had to rush to get changed, with no time to develop the notorious 'Wembley nerves'. Manager Scot Symon told them, 'Just play normally' . . . but that was the one thing they could not do, for the match had been taken out

of the context of their normal lives. It struck Docherty
as significant that WBA did not make the same mistake,
and actually trained on the morning of the match.

It was a lesson he was to remember when his own career
in management came along.

This is how the match was reported on the Monday:

FA Cup Final 1954
West Bromwich Albion 3 Preston North End 2
from The Times of May 3 1954

The pages of history were turned back at Wembley
Stadium on Saturday when West Bromwich Albion,
emerging from their dark cloud of recent weeks, cast
down Preston North End at the last breath to win the
FA Cup for the fourth time by three goals to two.

So the years 1888 and 1954 held hands. For just as
the mighty 'invincibles' of Proud Preston were thwarted
by a local band of players from the Midlands at that
far distant year, watched by an astonished crowd of
record proportions – 17,000 strong! – standing around
the touchlines of Kennington Oval, so now once more
were the Lancastrians confounded in the presence of
Queen Elizabeth the Queen Mother and 100,000 spectators, ranged about the steep banks of Wembley's
elliptical bowl.

Thus the trophy returns to an old home at the Haw-
thorns to spend the coming months not far from the spot

where once its grandfather – the original 'little tin idol' – was stolen from a shop window in Birmingham, never to be seen again after the night of September 11, 1895. But that is another tale, and one, let it be hoped, that will never be repeated.

And now the season's account is settled, with Staffordshire the champions of the country. Side by side they can proudly present the FA Cup, the League Championship trophy at Wolverhampton near by, and the Shield of the third division (north) in the hands of Port Vale, nestling among the stark kilns of the potteries. With the second-division title going to Leicester, the major jewels in the English game girdle the waist of the British Isles, whither the rest of the country are left to cast envious and admiring glances.

Every Cup final is a good one for the victors. It is a great spectacle, too, a ceremony slowly built up, with its massed bands of the Scots and Irish Guards in scarlet jackets, the voice of a nation in its community singing, the solemn rendering of the hymn 'Abide With Me' and the arrival of royalty. If all else should happen to pall, the setting itself is rich and of a shining green texture, though for the first time that one can remember there were touches of brown in the Wembley pitch to tell of the lack of rain over the past weeks.

The light rain that fell for a while in the morning had no sort of effect on a playing surface which seemed to surprise both sides – and especially Preston – by its pace. Had the heavens opened 24 hours earlier, as they did when it was all over, we might have had a different story to tell, for Preston, in particular, like soft going. As it was, their short, delicate passing, seldom found its right groove or control, and often looked less effective than the long game of the Albion.

West Bromwich Albion in the end deserved their narrow triumph, though at one time it seemed very much as if the afternoon was about to slip from their control. They deserved it because of their morale and fighting spirit that brought them out of a forbidding future in the last half-hour.

Indeed, it was towards the end that one caught fleeting glimpses of the power that once was theirs, as an old confidence slowly began to course through their veins once more after so many recent disappointments. As they fought themselves out of a hole – inspired largely by Barlow at a critical phase – so this confidence grew until it began gently to pervade the whole side. It came not a moment too soon as the plain run of events will show.

First, Allen put Albion ahead at the twenty-first minute, but within 60 seconds Preston were level. Seven minutes after half-time Preston went into the lead with a goal that was disputed for offside, just as Dewhurst's goal for the North End at the Oval 66 years earlier had been disputed. This would have been enough to knock the stuffing out of any side, especially one that has borne so much hardship of late. But Albion caught a second wind just as Preston, with some precise bouts of short passing in the old Scottish style, for a moment seemed to be heading for revenge. But two goals in the last 25 minutes saw West Bromwich home once more.

The afternoon really was decided down the right flank of the Preston attack, where Finney on the day failed to prove himself the expected match winner. Certainly he produced a number of his wonderfully controlled dribbles – one of some 80 yards in length from end to end – but he was never incisive enough. Never once could he produce the odd man over, for Millard who played him really splendidly at left back, was expertly covered by Dugdale, Barlow, Dudley, and Kennedy elsewhere.

In fact, so well were Foster, Wayman, Baxter and Morrison shepherded that Finney often was forced into holding on longer than he wished. Finney, as it proved, on this occasion lacked the stature and the presence of Matthews who last year was able finally to take events and mould them to his own pattern.

If Preston then lost because Finney proved not to be the trump card as expected, and because the close passing and final incision near goal of Wayman, Baxter, and Foster were weak, West Bromwich got home through the gathering strength of their half-back line. Barlow, watchful and restrained until that last decisive phase, together with Dugdale and Dudley as a unit, finally held a greater authority than Docherty, Marston, and Forbes, though Docherty hunted the ball tirelessly and efficiently from beginning to end.

Allen, too, at centre forward, well supported by the thrust of Ryan and Lee, proved an important factor not only for his two goals but because of his intelligent mobility. He has a cool brain and an eye for a decisive move, and altogether proved a thorn in the Preston side. But all these were individual successes. In a largely defensive match – in spite of the five goals – there was little flowering team work except in spasms.

This was shown well enough in the untidy way most of the goals arrived. The first, for instance, was a Preston defensive error. Cunningham, trying to find Finney with a clearance, instead cannoned the ball straight at Lee, who, winning the rebound, flashed the ball square across goal for Allen to push it into an empty net.

Within seconds, however, Preston replied properly as Docherty, taking Finney's back pass, centred swiftly from the right for Morrison to head home into the far top corner. So it was 1–1 at half-time, though just before the interval both Docherty, after a tortuous dribble by his captain, and then Finney himself fired hopelessly wide from open positions.

The second half held what drama there was to be had. At the seventh minute ground passing between Docherty, Foster, and Wayman sent the centre forward clean through. He looked offside. The Albion defence stood idle. Wayman, alone in the world, dribbled past Sanders to hit the ball home almost playfully. But the whistle never blew. The referee and the linesman were satisfied. It was a goal, which somehow seemed quite unreal. Now Preston were ahead and for a spell the Albion seemed doomed as Finney indulged in a few trills, ineffective though they proved.

But with 25 minutes left the turning point arrived as Barlow suddenly arose with raking stride to lift Albion out of the mire. Crashing through on one of his dribbles he appeared to collide with Docherty inside the penalty area, and there was Allen the next moment preparing to take a penalty kick. It was a situation to test the strongest nerve, and though his shot was swift and low Thompson, getting his hand to the ball, almost made a miraculous save. Yet many wondered about the decision.

As the hands of the clock moved on the Albion grew stronger. Their long passing game held the greater threat. But extra time seemed a certainty until, with two minutes left, Kennedy – who showed the value of experience in his strange position of right back – found Ryan with a ground pass. Griffin, cutting in at full pace to take Ryan's chip, flicked the ball past Walton with his head and shot home low across Thompson's body to the far corner. It was all over, and soon Millard, with the cup held aloft, was being chaired off the field. West Bromwich at last had some reward for the season.

West Bromwich Albion: Sanders; Kennedy, Millard; Dudley, Dugdale, Barlow; Griffin, Ryan, Allen, Nicholls, Lee

Preston North End: Thompson; Cunningham, Walton; Docherty, Marston, Forbes; Finney, Foster, Wayman, Baxter, Morrison

Docherty had quickly become a firm favourite with the fans at Preston North End. The teenager from the slums of Glasgow who had survived on handouts and borrowed football boots was going places. A Jaguar car, large club house, good money and new suits illustrated sharply the first real taste of the good life.

The fans soon realised that the talkative young Scot would spare no effort in his determination to make an impact on results and to help Preston become a footballing force again after a lean time in the second division. Tom Finney, Preston's captain, who played on the right wing in front of Docherty, admired his wholehearted involvement in every game: 'He was a tremendous player and never pulled any punches, even on the training ground. It was like having a juggernaut behind me in the team. He was a relentless competitor throughout a game and a man to have on your side.' Later he was to describe him as one of the hardest tacklers, and one of the best passers of a ball, he had ever seen on a football field.

It was Docherty's all-action approach and will to win that first alerted the Scottish selectors. He had been a reserve for his country several times before breaking into the team for his first cap, but the self-motivating Docherty had sustained his belief that his chance would eventually come to prove himself at the highest level.

An additional incentive was to replace the man holding down Scotland's regular right-half position, Bobby Evans. It was Evans who had kept him out of the Celtic team and was responsible for Docherty's belief that he had little alternative but to try first-team football with Preston; two years later he was dramatically named in the Scotland team for his first cap, against Wales at Hampden Park in November 1951. His selection was all the sweeter because the man he replaced was Bobby Evans. He recalls clearly the proud moment he was picked for his country. The Preston team were in Morecambe relaxing by the sea before an important League game.

> The first I knew about it was when a local newspaper reporter rang the hotel where we were staying to ask me for my reaction to being picked. At first I thought it was someone playing a game, then it sank in that he was telling the truth.

Like all true Scots, Docherty has a special place in his heart for Hampden Park. His first visit had been eight years before, when he was fifteen, and the memory of its impact has stayed with him even today. It was a wartime match, against England. The involvement of the crowd was what struck him most. They seemed as much a part of the team as the players themselves. Every time the ball went in the air they seemed to will it towards a Scotsman; when a Scottish player challenged for the ball they tensed as if to help him. Later he was to find that not even a Wembley crowd gave their team such support. There, when a goal was scored, anyone outside the ground would not know from the noise whose it was. But, as he puts it, 'stand outside Hampden when Scotland score and your instinct is to find an air raid shelter – the sound is an explosion of joy.'

His mother Georgina and his friends from his days at Celtic were at Hampden Park for his début on 28 November. He was nervous and keyed up, eager to impress and to establish himself in the Scotland team. He collected every newspaper report of the game which showed that Scotland's right-half was . . . Docherty. The team was Cowan in goal, Young and Cox the full-backs, Docherty, Woodburn and Forbes the half-back line, and the forwards Waddell, Orr, Reilly, Steel and Liddell.

> The experienced internationals like Willie Waddell and Billy Liddell helped me to settle in. I was trembling in the dressing-room before the game but they helped to calm me down. I will never forget that famous Hampden roar when we ran onto the pitch and the feeling of pride that I was at last a fully-fledged Scotland player in my own right.

After a tentative start, as he accustomed himself to the big occasion, Docherty was quickly into his stride, tackling hard and pressing forward to help his forwards in the style of adventurous power play the Preston fans knew so well. In the opening minutes he surged forward to the edge of the Welsh penalty area and unleashed a fierce drive which had the Wales keeper Shutt making a fine save. Reports of the match were unanimous in saying that Docherty had an outstanding second half with his sharp tackling and intelligent distribution, especially when sweeping the ball out to the wings to try to upset the Welsh defensive pattern.

An Allchurch goal in the closing minutes snatched a narrow victory for Wales, and though disappointed with the result Docherty felt he had played well enough. It was a view endorsed by the Welsh left-winger that day, Roy

Clarke, who would be a regular opponent of Docherty's for his club side Manchester City. 'He was fearless in the tackle and gave all-out effort. I knew after his first tackle on me that I was in for a tough game. He was very hard but always fair.'

Despite the favourable press reports and congratulations from his team-mates the Scottish selectors promptly dropped Docherty and brought back the Portsmouth half-back Jimmy Scoular who had vied with Celtic's Bobby Evans and Ian McColl of Rangers for the Scotland No.4 shirt before Docherty had gained his first cap in the right-half position. For the next eighteen months Scoular was a consistent performer for Scotland, and Docherty's international future appeared to be fading as six games went by without him being given a second chance. Undaunted, he knew that hard work and faith in himself was the only way to stay in international contention and he continued to play at the top of his form for Preston. Another chance came in April 1953 when he was named for the game against England at Wembley. It was a second chance that he would grab with both hands as he became a regular in the Scotland team over the next eight years.

In the Scotland team that day at Wembley was Bobby Johnstone, the little ball-playing wizard from Hibernian. Johnstone, like Welshman Roy Clarke, would eventually join Manchester City and oppose Docherty often at club level during the 1950s. He remembers Docherty's style: 'You could tell straightaway that he was a fierce competitor. He was hard in the tackle and very determined, always looking for the ball and getting involved as much as he could. It was obvious he was going to be a very good player.'

The game with England ended in a 2–2 draw, Laurie Reilly, another forward from Hibernian, scoring the equalising goal in the closing seconds. The following month the selectors brought back Bobby Evans for the international with Sweden at Hampden. It convinced Docherty that he had finally established himself in the eyes of the selectors when Evans was named at right-half with Docherty switched to the left: 'Evans had always kept me out at Celtic and with Scotland. When I was named in the same team I knew I had definitely arrived at last as a Scotland player.' Sweden won the game 2–1, and Docherty was out of the team again for the next three internationals as the selectors gave Evans an extended run and tried Cowie and Aitken in the No.6 jersey. It didn't work and Docherty was back at right-half against Norway in the 1–0 victory at Hampden and the 1–1 draw in Oslo the following game.

During 1954 Docherty was to gain six international caps and also play his first World Cup games. He appeared first against Austria in Zurich in a match Scotland were expected to find far beyond them; instead, with a little luck, they might easily have won. Austria opened the scoring with a goal which Docherty maintains to this day should not have been allowed – he says the television pictures clearly showed that the ball had not crossed the line. In the second half Scotland set about redressing the scoreline with tremendous gusto, so much so that in face of their determined tackling the more experienced Austrians could put few passes together; the half-back line of Docherty, Davidson and Cowie afterwards came in for special mentions in a number of press reports.

Unfortunately the Austrians, probably out of frustration, began playing the man rather than the ball, with the result that Scotland got very few chances to equalise. Even so the Austrian goalkeeper was forced into a desperate save close to the end, gathering the ball right on his line only at the second attempt.

Scotland's international standing had never been higher than after that match; three days later in Basle it was to plunge to its lowest. Mighty Uruguay, who had entered the World Cup twice before – in 1930 and 1950 – and won it each time had no thoughts of experiencing their first-ever defeat in the competition and made sure by trouncing the Scots 7–0. In a temperature associated more with the Sahara than with Switzerland, Scotland at first won their full share of the ball and twice nearly scored. The sheer speed of Uruguay's wingers told, however, and in seventeen minutes they opened the scoring.

By half-time it was 2–0 to Uruguay which was not really a true reflection of Scotland's play. On the resumption, though, the Uruguayans moved up first one gear and then a second, until they were scoring almost at will and Scotland were out of the competition.

Four months later, however, they were back on a winning path with a 1–0 victory over Wales in Cardiff, but in December 1954 Docherty was to get another sharp reminder of the gulf between British and Continental players when Scotland were beaten comfortably 4–2 by the Hungarians at Hampden. 'They didn't play as many games as we did but they were exceptionally skilful. I remember thinking after watching the Hungarians that if I ever went into management I would want to have players like that.'

Three more caps followed in 1955 as he built on his growing international reputation, although he grimaces when he recalls the first of them in April against England at Wembley. His attention was particularly drawn to the man in front of him in the England No. 6 shirt. It was the teenage powerhouse half-back Duncan Edwards who was to lose his life so tragically three years later after being fatally injured in the Munich air crash. 'Young Duncan had everything. He tackled like an ox, could pass the ball, head it accurately and shoot with power. Even at that age you could see he was something special.' Docherty remembers the game for the result as well. England won 7–2 with Docherty preventing England's biggest win over the old enemy when he scored his first goal for his country.

The following month the Scots bounced back in Vienna when they beat Austria 4–1, although the end of the month saw the team given another lesson by the Hungarians as they went down in Budapest as Docherty earned his twelfth cap.

During 1957 he not only enjoyed his longest spell in the Scotland team, gaining eight further caps including four World Cup games, but also received the accolade of the captaincy. The first qualifying match was against

Switzerland in Basle, scene of the débâcle four years previously against Uruguay. This time the weather was more European and the result was more acceptable as Scotland won 2–1. Even so, the Swiss scored after just twelve minutes and went on to control the first half with only Docherty capable of showing much resistance.

Early in the second half a controversial corner allowed Scotland to equalise. Then the heavy, rain-sodden pitch began to take its toll on the part-time Swiss players, but the Scots still lacked any real penetration. They hung on, however, showing just one flash nearing full-time to grab the lead.

This is how James Leatherdale has recorded that match in his book *Scotland's Quest for the World Cup:*

Switzerland 1 Scotland 2
at Basle, Sunday May 19 1957

In the World Cups of the 1950s and 1960s competing nations saw nothing wrong with cramming in fixtures in as short a period as possible. Today, it is uncommon to find a country playing two World Cup qualifiers inside a month. In 1957 Scotland completed their first three in a space of nineteen days. World Cup eliminators were contested in Basle and Madrid, with a friendly in West Germany in between.

Switzerland had already taken a point off Spain, who were now in desperate straits following the loss of two more at Hampden. A Scottish win in Basle would put

Scotland three points out in front, with one foot propping open the door to Sweden. Whether or not they achieved this victory depended in large measure on the mood of their hosts, historically – like their Central European neighbours Austria and Hungary – one of the most fluctuating of continental sides. At their best the Swiss were acclaimed tactical innovators: at their worst – not surprising with part-timers – one of Europe's weaker units.

When Tommy Docherty stepped out into the St Jakob's Stadium he could have been forgiven haunting memories of the last time he had done so. But now the opponents were Switzerland, not Uruguay; and the weather filthy, not scorching. Hopefully, Docherty was not too sensitive about the colours he was wearing, for it appeared that the Scotland team were resorting to optical skullduggery. The match was being transmitted on Eurovision (the second half live to Scotland) and in those days of black and white pictures the Swiss strip of red and white was not easily distinguishable from the Scots' blue and white. Switzerland requested that Scotland change their strip but none other was available. The hosts then provided a set of their own, but if the players had hopes of providing football as dazzling as their appearance, the Swiss had other ideas. Scotland were a goal behind after just twelve minutes. Caldow had tried to bring it about earlier, but his two suicidal back-passes had been retrieved. Now, Vonlathen despatched the ball to Meier, whose fast, low, return pass was thrashed past Younger from fifteen yards.

The goal was no more than Switzerland deserved. The home side did not appear inconvenienced by the chilly, heavy atmosphere or the sodden pitch, and for most of the opening half were in unquestioned control of the match. Meier, Ballaman and Schneiter slowed the pace of the game to their wishes, assisted by the sight of their opponents regularly being dumped on their backsides from unsure footing, and encouraged by Younger fumbling almost everything that came his way. Docherty stood out as the one Scot most capable of resisting the home side.

The change in Scotland's fortunes began twelve minutes from half-time. It owed everything to a corner awarded in error and Mudie's massive header which flashed past the groping Parlier. It was as well that the Scottish viewing public had not been privy to the first-half performance, for they would not have been comforted. The second period was little better, except that the Swiss had now run out of steam – the clinging pitch having its effect on part-time legs. Even so, the Scottish attack – Mudie excepted – was singularly bereft of penetration. The team was left to rejoice at one flash of inspiration nineteen minutes from time. Collins dived to meet Smith's corner and flicked the ball beyond Parlier to wedge in the far stanchion.

There was still time for Collins's defenders to attempt hara-kiri, as when McColl's back-pass was clutched by Younger down at the far post with inches to spare. Switzerland couldn't pull the game back, fluffing the chances which came their way. With the final whistle

Scotland possessed a final three-point lead at the halfway stage in their group, but the Scottish press were not in the mood for congratulations: 'Some Scottish players probably realised that they will never again play so badly and be on a winning side'.

Switzerland: Parlier; Kernen, Koch; Grobety, Frosio, Schneiter; Antenen, Ballaman, Vonlathen, Meier, Riva

Scotland: Younger (Liverpool); Caldow (Rangers), Hewie (Charlton Athletic); McColl (Rangers), Young (Rangers), Docherty (Preston North End); Smith (Hibernian), Collins (Celtic), Mudie (Blackpool), Baird (Rangers), Ring (Clyde)

A 3–1 victory over the reigning world champions West Germany was followed by a journey to Madrid where Docherty led his country to a sad 1–4 defeat. From the kick-off there was plainly only one side likely to win, Younger in goal being the sole factor preventing a rout. Scotland managed to salvage some sort of pride ten minutes from the end, but in the words of the report in the *Scotsman* newspaper Spain had 'played with them as a cat would a mouse'.

The national side had six months in which to gather themselves before their last and decisive qualifier, against Switzerland at Hampden Park. The Swiss impressed with their fluid and penetrating play, but it was the home side who opened the scoring when captain Docherty's pass allowed Robertson to side-foot the ball under the dive of the Swiss goalkeeper. Retaliation came quickly, the Swiss then began to surge forward leaving the Scots in something alarmingly close to disintegration.

With the score at 2–2, the end came amid controversy. After a scramble to clear the ball off their line, Scotland swept upfield and Scott found himself with the ball at his feet but obviously off-side. He hesitated and purely as a gesture put the ball into the net, fully expecting that play would be brought back. But the referee allowed the goal. The Swiss, understandably, were infuriated, but even then they came within an inch of equalising ten minutes before time. The record stood, however. Scotland had qualified; none too convincingly, but they were on their way to Sweden for the finals.

Docherty, temporarily at least, had lost his edge and took no part in the three matches before Scotland were eliminated. There were more caps for him in 1958, however, when he had left Preston for Arsenal, bringing his tally up to twenty-five in a sustained international career during which he had established himself as a world-class half-back.

3 A Hero at Highbury

As an established Scottish international wing-half, Docherty was now a hot property and attracting the attention of other leading clubs. Matt Busby was keeping an eye on him from Old Trafford, while Everton had actually offered Preston £16,000 – a big fee in those days – to take him to Goodison Park.

He had spent nine years at Deepdale and was happy there, but a club-or-country row was to break the bond with his first English club. The 1958 World Cup was held in Sweden, and Docherty was burning with ambition to play for Scotland in the finals. The new Preston manager Cliff Britton was equally adamant that he must go on the club's pre-season tour of South Africa. He ignored the club's demand and told Britton he was going to Sweden and would be leaving Preston when he returned.

The World Cup trip proved to be a disaster. We didn't win a single game and I didn't kick a single ball for Scotland [who could only draw with Yugoslavia, then lost to Paraguay and France]. So the row with Preston proved a futile one, although at the time I believed Cliff Britton could have allowed me to go to the World Cup with my country and join the club in South Africa afterwards. It's all very well in hindsight, but after the row I decided I must get away.

Preston tried to persuade him to change his mind but he was always uncompromising if he felt wronged. Reluctantly Britton left him out of the team for the opening game of the new season in August 1958 and replaced him with Gordon Milne who was to continue the great tradition of Preston half-backs by going on to gain England international honours. The significance of that opening game was that it was against Arsenal. After watching it Docherty was talking with friends in the car park when Britton walked up and asked if he still wanted to leave the club. When Docherty insisted, he was told to report to the office where Arsenal manager George Swindin wanted to speak with him.

Minutes later he was an Arsenal player, transferred for £27,000.

From Britton's point of view it was ideal. If Docherty had to move, he wanted him as far away as possible. He was well aware how popular he was with the Preston public, and did not want him on the doorstep magnetising the crowds away from Deepdale.

The Gunners had signed him to replace their injured skipper and England international, Joe Mercer, who had been at his peak either side of the Second World War. Soon Docherty was being proclaimed as the most inspirational player at Highbury since the great Mercer himself, and certainly he sparked off a revival in Arsenal's fortunes in the same way as the veteran had done before him. His debut came in a 3–0 win over Burnley at home within a week or two of his signing, and he made an immediate, if erratic, impact on the terraces.

The Arsenal fans found out straightaway that Docherty could talk a good game as well as play one. Indeed, after only forty-five minutes the boo-boys were in action. Arsenal had produced little fire in that first half, the main action being Docherty bawling and shouting instructions to his team-mates and pointing his finger to where he felt they should be positioned and who they should be marking. Shouts of 'Belt up, Docherty' and 'Shut your mouth, Docherty, and get on with the game' were coming from the frustrated fans as the team played through a goalless first half lacking in incident or excitement. Docherty was aware that the club had paid a big fee for him and knew a lot was expected of him and was even more determined when he ran out for the second half. Within minutes he won the ball with a strong tackle and measured a perfectly weighted pass through to inside-forward Jimmy Bloomfield which led to Arsenal's first goal. Now the fans were roaring approval of their new boy, and when his long-range shot deflected into the Burnley net for Arsenal's second goal he had won them over. Cliff Holton's third for Arsenal was the icing on the cake, but it was Docherty who had made the barrackers eat their words. A scorer on his debut and the inspiration behind the second-half surge by the team, he was clapped from the field by his team-mates and walked to the dressing-rooms to thunderous applause from the fans.

Docherty played another outstanding game for Arsenal that September, this time against Spurs, a match which was rapturously reported the following Monday:

**Arsenal 3 Tottenham Hotspur 1
from The Times of September 15 1958**

It was like the old days again at Highbury on Saturday, the days of one's youth, standing crushed high up on the terraces, awaiting the appearance of James and Bastin, Jack and Hulme.

The figures now are different, of course, but the old feeling was alive; one could sense it in the air of expectancy, almost of impatience, as a 65,000 crowd, white in its shirtsleeves under a dazzling Mediterranean sun, and compressed behind closed gates, awaited this battle of north London. Outside the ground at the day's start, mounted police took control and the ticket touts went away empty handed. Inside, at the day's end, it was Arsenal in complete charge and the Spurs who withdrew baffled.

The changing tides of football are quite unpredictable. Here are Arsenal, not so long ago a butt of the critics but now cock of the roost again, going great guns in attack with fifteen goals in their last three matches. Here are Tottenham, second and third in the Championship over the past two years, becalmed in dangerous waters with scarcely a puff of wind in their white sails. Yet both sides have virtually the same composition as last season. To find the deep roots for all this change may be a job for a psychoanalyst. But to the huge swaying crowd at least there were some powerful pointers to provide an answer.

First, of course, the arrival of Docherty at Highbury has given Arsenal the dynamic control at wing-half so lacking since the days of Mercer. He has infected the whole side, lifted the youthful Ward on his flank into a bright new world, and generally chivied the forwards in front of him into ceaseless activity. The team has responded as a complete unit, mixing a brand of short and long passing with such effective accuracy at the moment that they find themselves on a flood tide of success. This confidence has sprouted at the speed of mushrooms, with Clapton and Bloomfield showing dash and sharp footwork in attack and Herd supplying the lethal finish.

These, of course, are not the days of James, Bastin and company again, not by a long chalk, but it is all a fair enough substitute and in this vein, at least, Arsenal may take some dislodging, though they will still have to prove themselves when the going becomes difficult. Meanwhile, however, the golden touch has returned in some measure and its effect may be far reaching. A strong Arsenal is good for the game.

Equally apparent on the surface are the present causes of Tottenham's decline. For the past two seasons Blanch-flower and Harmer have been the nerve centre of their delicate machine. It has been a telling colourful partner-ship. It may be so again in due course for both are artists. But at the moment there is nothing beneath the velvet glove. Docherty now reduced the dainty little Harmer to anonymity while Blanchflower, bereft of his finer touches, seemed unable to change gear. He and Iley frequently were caught napping as wing-halves too far advanced so that Norman was left on occasion with his backs to patrol defensive deserts wide enough for a camel corps.

Arsenal, indeed, should have won far more handsomely and could have been four goals to the good by half-time. As it was, forty minutes sped by before Nutt spun home a miscued volley from Clapton's sizzling run and centre. At the change of ends Herd quickly delivered the first of two rockets from twenty yards to put Arsenal further ahead and to extinguish Tottenham's belated and spirited reply. That bright little flame was snuffed out imperiously. The executioner again was Herd as he crashed home an extravagant thunderbolt from outside the penalty area. It capped some juggling by Bloomfield and the whole concourse exploded.

Arsenal: Kelsey; Wills, Evans; Ward, Dodgin, Docherty; Clapton, Groves, Herd, Bloomfield, Nutt

Tottenham Hotspur: Hollowbread; Baker, Hopkins; Blanchflower, Norman, Iley; Medwin, Harmer, Smith, Clayton, Robb

Docherty quickly established himself as a firm favourite with the Arsenal supporters with a string of consistently high-quality performances that won over the hearts and minds of the Londoners. Soon after his debut he was again cheered from the field as Arsenal crushed by 6–1 the same Bolton team that only a few months earlier had beaten Manchester United in the FA Cup final. Docherty received rave notices for his part in the demolition, being described as the player who had marshalled the Arsenal defence, prompted the attacks and whose superb pass had laid on the fourth goal. The big fee paid for him was now accepted as money well spent.

His total commitment was underlined in November when he played for Scotland against Northern Ireland at Hampden Park and he offered to fly back after the international so that he could play that same night at Highbury against Juventus, the Italian giants. The gesture endeared him to the fans.

The combative, all-action style of Docherty, the player with a will to win above the call of duty, was soon to land him in trouble, however.

In the Boxing Day game at Luton he clashed with referee Ken Stokes as he left the pitch after the final whistle. Docherty, upset at decisions going against his team-mates which he felt lacked fairness, was reported by Stokes for using abusive language, a charge he strenuously denied when asking for a personal hearing. A three-man Football Association commission found him guilty, however, and the severity of the sentence – a two-week ban, heavy fine and the loss of his wages – was a cruel blow to Docherty's pride. He felt he had let down the supporters and the club. He was shocked by the punishment because it was his first challenge to authority in nearly ten years in English football during which time he had never been sent off.

The man to become known as a tough disciplinarian was quick to point out in the press that he was not a player who moaned about authority or discipline. It was a prophetic response when he added that his ambition was to move into coaching and management and he did not want to be given a reputation as a trouble-causer.

Before starting his ban Docherty was in the team that beat Colchester 4–0 in an FA Cup third round replay at Highbury before 62,000. Ruled out of the next two rounds, he signed off in typical style with another man-of-the-match performance acclaimed in the press reports. It was noted that, even when when the result was beyond doubt, he was urging colleagues to greater effort and stamping his authority on the game. It was a natural leadership style that led before long to his elevation to the captaincy whenever the regular skipper, Welshman Dave Bowen, was absent.

His last appearance before suspension was in a victory over Spurs in February 1959 at White Hart Lane. Critics drooled over Docherty's contribution in the 4–1 derby victory; 'one of the best performances from an Arsenal player in recent years', said one report. Docherty had linked up with Dave Bowen to take an iron grip on the game straight from the kick-off.

Even when Arsenal were reduced to ten men when forward Len Julians was sent off for allegedly kicking an opponent it was Docherty, shouting instructions and urging on his team-mates, who called for even greater action to maintain Arsenal's effort. One report summed him up as 'like a sergeant in the Light Brigade'.

Tommy Docherty, Preston's new recruit from Glasgow Celtic, 1949.

2 Docherty, with Tom Finney, both resplendent in Preston blazers.

3 The Preston side which lost to West Bromwich Albion in the 1954 FA Cup final. *Left to right*: Finney, Wayman, Baxter, Cunningham, Walton, Docherty, Foster, Forbes, Marston, Morrison, Mattinson and Thompson.

Docherty introduces Jimmy Murray of Scotland to the Duke of Gloucester before the start of the 1958 Scotland v England international at Hampden Park, won by England 4–0.

The Arsenal photo-call at the beginning of the 1959–60 season. *Top row, left to right*: Hinton, D. P. Clapton, Bacuzzi, Coe, Goy, McKechnie, Meldrum, Young, Goring; *second row*: Everitt, Snedden, Head, Dodgin, Kelsey, Standen, Mel Charles, McCullogh, Evans, Hughes; *third row*: Henderson, D. R. Clapton, Ward, Wills, Groves, Docherty, Bloomfield, Herd, Julians; *front row*: Goulden, Morton, Barnwell, O'Neill, Haverty, Magill, Nutt.

6 Docherty laps the Highbury stadium before the start of the 1960–61 season.

7 Leonardi, the Roma forward, is punched to the ground by Eddie McCreadie of Chelsea during the ill-tempered Inter-Cities Fairs Cup tie at Stamford Bridge in September 1965. McCreadie was sent off for that retaliatory punch.

When the Barcelona left-back, Eladio, was sent off, after an incident with John Hollins of Chelsea during the Inter-Cities Fairs Cup semi-final at Stamford Bridge in May 1966, extraordinary scenes ensued. Eladio refused to leave the field; four policemen took a hand; despite the pleas of the Barcelona captain, Muller (No. 8), Rife (No. 7) and Benitez (No. 2) the referee stuck to his decision, and after a long interval, Eladio eventually left the field.

9 Peter Osgood was one of Tommy Docherty's most brilliant discoveries during those early unforgettable years at Stamford Bridge. Here Osgood evades a Shrewsbury defender's tackle in the fifth round of the 1965–66 FA Cup, won by Chelsea 3–2, in front of 51,000 spectators. George Graham is in support.

10 Peter Bonetti makes a brilliant save from John Connelly in the Chelsea v Manchester United match at Stamford Bridge in March 1966 in front of a 60,000 crowd, which Chelsea won 2–0. In the picture, from left to right, are Marvin Hinton, Denis Law, Bobby Charlton, John Hollins, Connelly (almost obscured by Hollins) and Joe Kirkup.

11 Mutual congratulations: Tommy Docherty and Sir Matt Busby shake hands on the 1966 transfer of Alex Stepney from Chelsea to Manchester United after his single senior appearance for Chelsea.

2 Tony Hateley, brilliant in the air, less so on the ground, arrived at Chelsea from Aston Villa in October 1966. Here he scores a spectacular headed goal against Fulham at Craven Cottage soon after his arrival. It was Hateley who scored Chelsea's only goal against Leeds in the semi-final of the FA Cup that season which put Chelsea into the final against Spurs.

3 Chelsea's victory by 1–0 over Leeds United in the semi-final of the 1966–67 FA Cup took them at last to Wembley. Here Peter Lorimer shoots spectacularly for goal as Eddie McCreadie tries to block the shot.

14 Tommy Docherty hugs his No. 2, Alan Harris, after Chelsea had won through against Leeds in the 1966–67 FA Cup semi-final. Ron Harris, Alan's brother, is to the left of the embracing couple.

15 A clutch of Docherty's brilliant young 1966–67 team evidently unable to stop Geoff Hurst scoring for West Ham at Stamford Bridge. From left to right of those Chelsea players visible are Tony Hateley, John Boyle, Peter Bonetti, Marvin Hinton and Eddie McCreadie.

By now Docherty was becoming a folk hero at Highbury. In a draw at Birmingham more accolades flowed towards him in the match reports: 'Docherty gave another outstanding exhibition of half-back play' when he was the driving force as two Arsenal players limped through most of the game with injury. And when Manchester United's 'Busby Babes' visited Highbury unbeaten in their previous twelve games it was Docherty who orchestrated Arsenal's 3–2 victory with another display of power-tackling, timely interceptions cutting out the supply of ball to the United forward trio of Albert Quixall, Dennis Violett and Bobby Charlton, who had been in such good goal-scoring form before the Arsenal game.

Another game against Everton at Highbury, which produced an emphatic 3–1 Arsenal win, was to reveal another dimension to his range.

Bill Dodgin was injured and Docherty was asked to play centre-half, his position as a schoolboy player, and on a rock-hard frozen Highbury pitch he shut out the menace of Everton centre-forward Dave Hickson, the man nicknamed the 'Wild Bull'. Arsenal manager George Swindin was astonished at the display from his stand-in centre-half. He had gambled on Docherty's adaptability and declared afterwards, 'He had a blinder.' Injuries to key players were to cost Arsenal dearly in the Championship race and in the final game of the season at Highbury Docherty was again asked to play centre-half. He produced another outstanding performance in a 2–1 win over Birmingham. The style was the one he had started with in August 1958 . . . shouting advice to team-mates, tireless energy as he broke up attacks and moved forward to press home the advantage, and powerful tackling. When he left the field Docherty, after just one season at Highbury, was given a standing ovation.

The bargain buy from Preston had been the big-part player in Arsenal achieving third place in the Championship, their highest position since winning the title six years earlier.

In his second season at Arsenal (1959–60) Docherty's power play went on unchecked as he produced match-winning performances. The Gunners bought Welsh international Mel Charles for £45,000 – nearly double the fee they had paid Preston for Docherty – but Docherty responded with a matchless performance against Manchester City in a 3–1 victory at home. He was described as the 'complete wing-half', while the luckless Charles struggled to fit into the team. In October Docherty was eagerly awaiting the visit of his former team-mates from Preston. It was to prove a major disappointment. Twenty minutes into the game he moved to intercept a cross from the Preston right just as Bill Dodgin at centre-half challenged for the ball. Docherty crashed to ground, his ankle broken in a freak clash with his team-mate. The first man at his side was his old friend and colleague Tom Finney, the Preston skipper. Within twenty-four hours, his leg in plaster, Docherty was declaring he would be fit to play in two months.

The 1960–61 season would be his last at Arsenal. Manager George Swindin wanted to buy George Eastham from Newcastle United and, to help finance a deal, was willing to sell Docherty to Blackpool. Docherty had made it a mission as a player not to be pushed around on the field and was now in no mood to be pushed around off it: 'If I can't play for Arsenal I'll hang up my boots. It's as simple as that,' he told his Arsenal bosses in his usual shoot-from-the-hip manner.

In February 1961, two and a half years after joining the club, Docherty played his last game for Arsenal, at Newcastle. His Highbury days had been irrevocably soured by events, but in any case fate was dealing him a fresh hand. Across London, at Stamford Bridge, Chelsea wanted a coach to help manager Ted Drake. Walter Winterbottom, the FA's head of coaching, had recommended him and Burnley's Jimmy Adamson as the best men available, and within days Docherty was saying goodbye to his many friends at Arsenal with a letter in his pocket offering him the job at Stamford Bridge on wages of £30 a week.

That was the end of Tommy Docherty's playing days. He did turn out a few times for Chelsea when they were in a jam, but at the age of 32 and playing as well as ever, an outstanding career, begun in 1948, had to all intents and purposes ended . . . characteristically, if not in a full-blown storm, at least in a stiff squall.

4 Chelsea: Crossing the Bridge

Outspoken, opinionated and supremely confident in his own ability, Docherty was caught unawares by Arsenal's move to show him the door. A sense of disillusionment set in, but in any case he was losing his enthusiasm for playing and wanted to try coaching and management.

He was in luck. The Chelsea team were treading water in the middle of the first division and the directors were known to be impatient for change. The ageing manager Ted Drake, legendary centre-forward for Arsenal and England, was becoming desk-bound and losing the essential daily touch with his players; indeed the training pitch had become almost a no-go area for him. The club were desperate for a younger, track-suited man who could deal direct with the playing staff and bring on the young talent at Stamford Bridge.

So on the whole Docherty was pleased when Arsenal's George Swindin gave him his blessing to apply for the coaching job at the Bridge. His letter was posted the same night; and five days later he was in charge of the Chelsea coaching staff. His interview in the Chelsea boardroom had been brief and humorous. It was also straight to the point.

The chairman Joe Mears [who ironically had been
on the FA Committee hearing Docherty's case in
the Stokes complaint two years earlier] told me he
knew nothing about football. He then waved his hand
towards the other directors and said, 'And this lot
know a damn sight less.'

The banter suited the wise-cracking Docherty: 'There's
a lot of them about,' he joked back. An instant bond had
been formed that was to keep them close friends until Joe
Mears's premature death some years later. When asked
when he could start work at the Bridge Docherty was
ready: 'I started the moment I signed my letter applying,'
he told Mears.

Arsenal let their Scottish firebrand join Chelsea without a fee, although they insisted on one important
proviso: if he turned out in the Chelsea colours they
would have to pay Arsenal £200 a game.

In fact I played four times for Chelsea before stopping
altogether, so Arsenal finished up with an extra 800
quid in the bank. I can say sincerely that I enjoyed my
playing days at Arsenal and I will always be grateful
to them for the way they helped me get my start in
management.

The initial confession by Joe Mears, albeit tongue in
cheek, that he and his board knew nothing about football
encouraged Docherty, who prefers working on his own
and making his own decisions without interference. He
felt immediately that he was starting off on the right foot,
but soon came out of the clouds with a reminder from

Ted Drake at their first formal meeting that he was not the man he wanted. Vic Buckingham, an old pal from their days in the forces, had been his choice, but at least he made it clear that he had nothing personally against Docherty.

This was not the most encouraging of starts, but in the few weeks left of the 1960–61 season Docherty was to demonstrate the quick-fire repartee and sharp decision-making that were to characterise his career. He was close to the players and a good motivator. Mears and his directors, quietly monitoring the situation after his arrival, were impressed.

The season ended modestly, however, with the team in mid-table after being dismissed from the FA Cup at the first hurdle 1–2 at home to lowly Crewe Alexandra in front of more than 32,000 disbelieving spectators. They may not have pulled up any trees in the unspectacular early weeks of Docherty's career at Stamford Bridge, but he knew the potential at the club was breathtaking.

The Chelsea youngsters had retained the FA Youth Cup with an avalanche of goals. Fulham were overwhelmed 9–0 before Oxford United suffered 7–0 as the competition was dominated by the Chelsea apprentices. It made Docherty sharply aware of the quality throughout the club. When he says they had the best young players in the business and were the envy of other clubs and their scouts, it makes good sense. Talent was everywhere in the team, from goalkeeper Peter Bonetti to Bobby Tambling, Barry Bridges and the Harris brothers Alan and Ron, not to mention the brilliant Terry Venables. And there was another player at the Bridge whom Docherty rated the best finisher in European football.

> Jimmy Greaves was a man with golden boots. I tell you this: if Greavesie had stayed at Chelsea instead of going to Italy I'm sure we would have dominated English football. When you look at the number of those young players who became full internationals it was a great pity Greavesie didn't stay with us. There was no one to touch him here or on the Continent when it came to scoring goals. His goals would have made all the difference. I was choked when he left for Italy. The irony was that he needn't have gone, anyway. [Within a few weeks of Greaves succumbing to the lure of the lire Jimmy Hill had led the players in a successful campaign to have the maximum wage lifted.] If he had hung on a little longer with us we could have matched anything AC Milan were prepared to pay him. We could have given him what we felt he was worth to us, and I can tell you that was a lot of money with his goal-scoring ability.

Even more annoying, it was only a few short months later that Greaves returned to England and signed for Tottenham Hotspur. Docherty was devastated.

> I didn't have enough power when I first arrived at Chelsea to do anything to prevent Jimmy leaving us. Ted Drake was in charge and I was the coach responsible to him. Then the club blundered in my view when it was made known Greavesie wanted to come home. The club decided to send our secretary John Battersby to Milan to try and persuade him to come back to Chelsea. It was a big mistake. John was a fine secretary but not the man to go. I could have

talked to Jimmy as a player. I understood players and was convinced if I had gone to Milan I would have brought him back to Chelsea.

The move of Greaves to Italy may have devastated Docherty, but it also accelerated the demise of Ted Drake. He was already losing the support of the directors and spent the summer of 1961 searching desperately for a replacement for Greaves. Added pressure was put on him when Greaves played his last game in Chelsea's colours against the team he was about to join, AC Milan. The situation was haunting him and there seemed nothing he could do about it. Salvation appeared to be at hand, however, when the classy George Eastham had a row over terms with Arsenal. Docherty tried to strike while the iron was hot.

I appealed to George as an Arsenal old boy myself. It might have worked but he was offered a new contract by Arsenal and accepted. But I didn't think Ted Drake would have survived even if we had persuaded George to join us. Drake wasn't flavour of the month with the directors and it really was only a matter of time, I felt. In any case, losing out on Eastham moved him one step nearer the door.

By now Drake was clearly a man out of luck. In the opening match of the 1961–62 season the Chelsea captain Peter Sillett broke his leg. Drake moved for a replacement quickly enough, but Huddersfield Town's England full-back Ray Wilson, who went on to win a World Cup-winners medal in 1966, rejected the move south: another blow for Drake. Renewed optimism came when Bobby Tambling started scoring goals regularly, including a gem which helped Chelsea to beat Manchester United at the Bridge. But the fade-out for the team was equally dramatic, with just two wins in the opening six games despite the efforts of Tambling.

Desperate for a good performance with the rumblings from the boardroom getting louder by the match, Drake decided to gamble and asked Docherty, still very fit and in daily training, to start playing again in the hope that his vast experience would steady the young team. He asked him to play at left full-back in the next game against Sheffield United and astounded his critics by dropping his precociously talented teenager, Terry Venables. It paid off handsomely as Chelsea thrashed Sheffield United 6–1, with Bobby Tambling scoring a hat-trick. The gathering gloom had been lifted temporarily but the victory, though providing the spark, failed to ignite a revival. Two further defeats and a draw signalled the end. With four years of his ten-year contract still to run, Drake was sacked, helped on his way with a record golden handshake.

So it was that in September 1961, Tommy Docherty at just 33 became the youngest manager in the first division and came into his true kingdom. A few weeks later he was to be joined by Dave Sexton as his assistant and their highly successful partnership began. Eventually Sexton would succeed Docherty as manager just as he would succeed him at Manchester United in 1977.

The extrovert Scot who courted publicity contrasted sharply with Drake in his methods.

I was willing to give my opinion and meet the press. If something needed saying about Chelsea then I was not afraid to say it. But Ted was like Howard Hughes – his telephone number was ex-directory so nobody could speak to him. You couldn't run so much as a prison like that.

Docherty was told to prove himself before Christmas. He proved very little, for by then the team were bottom of the table. It might have looked grim but Docherty knew that there was the potential at the club to achieve success. It was a question of whether the directors would decide on a clean sweep of everything, including himself. He got his answer in emphatic fashion early in the new year.

We were preparing to leave Stamford Bridge for a Cup-tie at Liverpool. I'd decided to take the players for a break at the seaside and booked a hotel in Blackpool. I thought a working break by the sea would lift them for Anfield where we would need all the luck we could get. As the team coach was about to pull away from the ground for Euston station one of the office staff ran across to intercept it and told me the acting chairman, Charles Pratt, wanted to see me straightaway. A buzz went round the coach. The lads obviously felt – as I did – that this could be the bullet. I braced myself and walked into the chairman's office. You can imagine how I felt when he said the board felt I was doing a good job and we were on the right lines, and asked if I wanted the job on a permanent basis. When it sank in what he was saying, he asked me about terms. I told him money didn't bother me. I just wanted to get on with the job. When I got back to the coach, the players were silent. They thought

> I was going to say goodbye after being sacked. I sat
> down in my usual seat at the front then shouted,
> 'Right lads, from now on it's *Mr* Docherty. They
> started booing.'

The tie was lost, but Liverpool were glad to hear the
final whistle as they clung on to a 4–3 lead after Chelsea's
attacking, flowing football had won them many friends.

Undaunted by the Anfield Cup defeat, Docherty turned
his thoughts to the fight against relegation. The young
team – seven of them still in their teens – was performing
wonders for him, but the fact was that of his first ten
games in charge they lost eight. The talent was there,
but plainly the relegation battle was getting to them;
behind them was the history of a great club that had
been in the top flight for more than thirty years, and
to the supporters the very thought of going down was
unthinkable. It was a burden, and the search began for
experience to back up the talent.

Docherty turned to his native Scotland for inspiration.
Time was running out on the season and he needed new
players quickly. His immediate targets were two Arbroath
players, one a defender and the other a strong-tackling
midfield man, but it was a defender in their opposition
that day who caught his eye. The East Stirling full-back,
Eddie McCreadie, was summed up by Docherty as 'a
rough diamond but a gem of a player'. He proved to be an
outstanding player for Chelsea, forming with Ken Shellito
probably the best full-back pairing in the League.

The trip home was to earn Docherty the title of 'McChelsea' by those who felt he favoured Scottish players; but he insists that he judged them on merit. At all events he decided to keep faith with his team and that McCreadie would be his only signing that season. But the unthinkable happened and Chelsea dropped down to division two.

Expecting the sack, Docherty acted on the premise that attack is the best form of defence and recommended his directors to give every player a rise for their efforts during the season. To his astonishment they agreed and gave everyone £5 a week extra.

His first full season as manager began in August 1962, and his game plan was to win promotion at the first attempt. But first his managerial qualities were to be tested: before a ball was kicked a player's rebellion broke out when Peter Brabrook, Andy Malcolm, Mel Scott and Mike Harrison flatly refused their new contract terms. The Chelsea board, in particular his mentor the chairman Joe Mears, watched the situation with added interest. Docherty reacted in characteristic style, throwing three of them out of the club there and then, whilst Mike Harrison played just one more game before he too was sent packing.

Having quelled the mutiny Docherty then captured the imagination of the supporters and raised eyebrows in the boardroom by making Bobby Tambling captain. He was only 20 but in such a young team he was one of the old boys. The move was to pay rich dividends. The emphasis on youth breathed new life throughout the club, and the team led the second division at Christmas and was flowing easily towards the first. At the turn of the year the youngsters were pulling the pack along on a 7-point lead. Docherty purred with self-satisfaction. However, the smile on his face was frozen when on Boxing Day deep snow covered the country. Temperatures plummeted as an arctic winter settled in for weeks on end and brought football virtually to a halt. In fact the season had to be extended to make up the lost time. At Stamford Bridge they brought in bulldozers, tractors and even appealed to the army for help, but it was hopeless. The pitch was rock hard.

The momentum had been cruelly halted and Docherty could only watch helplessly, realising that the consequences could be severe for his team's promotion charge.

Eventually, though, temperatures rose, the snows melted and grounds improved. But Docherty's fears were justified when the team started playing again, for they lost a string of games and slipped from the leadership of the second division. He found himself praying for the snow again. Searching for an answer, he telephoned Joe Mears, on holiday in the south of France, and asked for permission to spend £45,000 on Derek Kevan, the big West Bromwich Albion forward.

It was a mistake. Kevan didn't take kindly to my
training routines. He thought I was a cross between
a prison warder and a regimental sergeant-major. He
mistook discipline for dictatorship. But he did play
one vital game for me, and it was a key factor in our
promotion.

Chelsea were still well on the promotion path until the second week in May when Stoke City, at one stage earlier in the season a dozen points behind, visited Stamford Bridge and, inspired by the veteran maestro Stanley Matthews, won 1–0 to make themselves the favourites with Sunderland to gain promotion. A glance at the table showed Docherty just how perilous was his team's position. Sunderland led the table on 52 points with one game left at home against Chelsea, who were 4 points behind them. Stoke, with two games left, were 3 points clear of Chelsea in second place. The mathematics were simple: Chelsea had to win their final two games at Sunderland and against Portsmouth to snatch promotion from Sunderland on goal average.

Docherty and his players headed for their north-east hotel three days before the vital game at Roker Park realising the enormity of their task. On top of everything else, Chelsea had not won away since Boxing Day. Docherty gave very serious thought to his tactics, and by match day had decided on drastic action.

The atmosphere, even as the teams arrived at the packed ground, was overpowering. From miles around the Sunderland fans had come to cheer their team to the Championship, and the noise reflected the fact. They knew all about Chelsea's open, flowing style, of course, but the lads could cope with that; and there was Chelsea's dreadful away record, too. There would be no problems, they thought. So let's get these ninety minutes over and then we can get on with the party.

Docherty's thoughts had come round to the belief that

this game was so crucial to his club's immediate future that he had to abandon his purist approach and pick a team that would roll up its sleeves and hit Sunderland hard and often. Accordingly, he dropped Graham Moore, Bert Murray and Barry Bridges and brought in the two toughest men on his books when it came to roughing up the opposition, Frank Upton and Derek Kevan. He also included the smallest man on Chelsea's books, Tommy Harmer, who was also one of the most skilful ball players at Stamford Bridge and a player he knew would trouble the big Sunderland defenders. Harmer's skill could be relied upon to hold possession and keep the Chelsea front players together.

In the dressing-room Docherty told Upton and Kevan that he wanted them to go in hard and knock Sunderland centre-half Charlie Hurley out of his stride. The ploy was put into action immediately from the kick-off when Upton ran straight at Hurley and barged into him as he tried to play the ball out of defence. The tone had been set. Momentarily the crowd were stunned. Then the mood changed; this was going to be war. Chelsea hunted ruthlessly for the ball, while Sunderland were further confused by Docherty switching his speedy winger Frank Blunstone over to the right and giving Bobby Tambling a wider role. It was Tambling's goals – thirty-five that season – that had kept Chelsea in contention for promotion. Just before half-time Harmer scored from Tambling's corner kick. And there was more drama to come.

During the break Docherty talked tensely to his players, telling them that they had to keep applying the pressure to defend the lead and not let them settle on the ball. The partisan crowd of over 60,000 were now angry, realising Docherty had not come to play fancy football but had drawn up a battle plan of 'win first, worry about reputation later'. By the time the match moved into injury time they were going wild as Sunderland poured men into the Chelsea penalty area. Docherty was off his bench screaming for his own men to get stuck in. Suddenly the ball ran into the path of Sunderland winger George Mulhall. A goal now would give Sunderland the promotion place and shatter Chelsea's season. But the final act of this remarkable game was a world-class save from Peter Bonetti, who hurled himself across goal to fingertip Mulhall's rocketing shot away from the top corner. Seconds later the final whistle blew, and Chelsea's players left the field to a cacophony of boos and catcalls from the incensed Sunderland supporters. A shamefaced Docherty later admitted it was not a game for fainthearts but insisted his tactics were right in the circumstances.

Kevan, the man who grimaced at Docherty's training routines, had done his job as one of the hard men of Roker Park, and then scored his only goal in seven games for Chelsea in the final match of the season against Portsmouth at Stamford Bridge. It started a rout as Bobby Tambling hit four in a 7–0 bombardment of Portsmouth who were outplayed from the start as Chelsea grabbed the runners-up spot, edged out Sunderland on goal average and won promotion back to the first division after just one year. Immediately afterwards Kevan was sold to Manchester City.

This is how *The Times* reported what was truly a match to remember for all Chelsea supporters:

Chelsea 7 Portsmouth 0
from The Times of May 9 1963

After one season of exile, Chelsea last night returned to the first division when they swamped Portsmouth in the final match of their season. They never seem to do things by halves. All they needed was a victory, and a 55,000 crowd arrived at Stamford Bridge expecting a night of twanging nerve and perhaps even defeat. Yet a goal in ninety seconds by Kevan – perhaps one of the most important he has scored and his first for Chelsea – relieved all the tension.

From that moment Chelsea unwound in a trice, could see the horizon of victory and swept through the night adding goal after goal. When the score was six, with still twenty-five minutes to go, the chant of the crowd was, 'We want seven'. And finally they got it when Tambling, having one of his great matches, crashed a rocket into the roof of the Portsmouth net for his own fourth goal.

So poor Sunderland, for the second year running, are left behind in the second division, now beaten on goal average. But there was no question about last night. With still four minutes left the pitch was invaded by practically every small boy in west London, probably mistaking the referee's whistle for a free-kick as full-time. For a brief moment there were visions of the match being abandoned through lack of discipline and Chelsea having to relive another night.

But sanity prevailed, the roar of the rest of the crowd of, 'Off, off, off' finally won through, and it was moments later when the young men could at last give vent to their feelings. The field became a human mass as the Chelsea players fought for their dressing-room. But Tambling, the captain and hero, was caught by the tide and tossed shoulder high like a blue fork in a turbulent sea.

It had been no match on a worn, brown field with an elusive ball. Yet one man mastered it, little Harmer, of the matchstick legs and the cool footballer's brain. He was the man who smoothed out any remaining fears that may have lurked after Kevan's early strike.

By the quarter hour Tambling cracked in number two from Blunstone's flick. At the half hour, in Greaves fashion, he went like a lizard through the grass, beating three men swiftly to plant his left-foot shot clearly beyond Armstrong. There it was at half time with Chelsea clearly well on course. Within half an hour of the second half four more goals had come. Superb pace, which left the defence standing, and a left-foot shot gave Tambling his third goal. Then a passage of interplay between Tambling and Blunstone gave Blunstone an opening. Next a penalty by Venables, after Brown had desperately pulled down Tambling, and finally that last thunderbolt from Tambling.

So we look back and see how Chelsea, once seven points ahead of this division, kept their cosmopolitan clans in suspense to the last. Now they can look forward, but if Kevan and Upton were used at the last as ramrods through the centre, they are not really what Chelsea will need in the first division.

Harmer, of course, remains the wise elder statesman, but his future in the top class is problematical. He is that sort of man, though, that Chelsea need in the years ahead, years that should see the emergence of Tambling, Shellito and Venables as real figures. As for Portsmouth, this night they were merely the other team.

Chelsea: Bonetti; Shellito, McCreadie; Venables, Mortimore, Ron Harris; Blunstone, Kevan, Upton, Harmer, Tambling

Portsmouth: Armstrong; Gunter, Wilson; Brown, Dickinson, Campbell; Barton, Gordon, Saunders, McCann, Lill

Docherty predicted that his young Chelsea team would be competing with the best in Europe within three years. His prediction was bang on target. Promotion was no fluke, either. The seeds of Chelsea's brilliant youth policy were beginning to bear large fruits as the burgeoning brilliance of those same youngsters was illustrated in that first season back in the top flight, in 1963–4, when they finished a highly respectable fifth behind the champions, Liverpool. At the start of the next, 1964–65, season thirty of the professionals on Chelsea's books (90 per cent) were under 25. The youngest was John Boyle at 17; John Hollins was a year older, Ron Harris was 19 and his brother Alan 21, the same age as Terry Venables and Bert Murray. The 'older' players included Peter Bonetti and Bobby Tambling, both 22, Barry Bridges 23 and defenders Eddie McCreadie and Ken Shellito who were 24. Docherty felt he needed just one piece to complete a title-winning jigsaw and paid just £5,000 for George Graham from Aston Villa. Graham was only 20 and had the height to give Chelsea that extra option Docherty was looking for in attack, where he felt Graham would be a big influence in opposing penalty areas.

These were heady days at Stamford Bridge, and Docherty introduced bonuses which would make his players some of the highest paid in the Football League if they were successful in the League and Cup competitions. 'We played attacking football and the lads were great to watch. They were quick, skilful and could run all day and they had a lot of individual flair. We had a magnificent team.'

All season the fans poured into the Bridge in record numbers to watch this entertaining young team which had proved it could compete with the best. It was to be a season that blazed with promise before exploding into volcanic controversy and abject disappointment.

5 Rocked at Blackpool

To bounce back to the top division so quickly, and with such a young team, and to have the fans flocking to watch your side wherever you went, speaks of a remarkable manager, so it is worth pausing to look at Docherty's methods and his tactics, and at his personality.

His passionate belief that individual physical fitness combined with hard work and discipline were the essential ingredients for success never wavered. It was a military style approach that tested a player's resilience, exposed weaknesses and on occasions provoked an unwillingess to respond to such a harsh regime. It made some believe they could climb mountains for Docherty and others that the training ground had become a drill field. Derek Kevan was one who thought Docherty's training methods smacked more of the parade ground than the playing field. Docherty felt Kevan was overweight and below peak fitness when he arrived at Stamford Bridge and the player cringed at his manager's attempts to knock him into shape.

Players with flair had formed an essential part of Docherty's creed ever since his boyhood days in Glasgow when he used to watch the great Scots teams of the day.

Celtic's flying winger Jimmy Delaney was one of his idols and left a lasting impression. At Preston the peerless Tom Finney nurtured and sustained Docherty's belief:

> In the teams I played for at Celtic, Preston and Arsenal we had pace on the wings. I believed that was the way the game should be played. Wingers were popular in those days, anyway. We played with just two men in midfield when I was at Chelsea, although critics felt it was surrendering the middle, but front players could easily fall back to cover any break from the opposition.

The formation of his team was essentially 4–2–4 with pace on the wings. He had quick, skilful, wide players such as Frank Blunstone and Bert Murray, then later Charlie Cooke and Peter Houseman. It worked and was attractive to watch, although the players realised it demanded the highest levels of fitness. It was a philosophy he continued at Rotherham and at Manchester United, where he brought in such exciting wing players as Steve Coppell and Gordon Hill, while Willie Morgan was already at the club when he arrived.

Dave Watson, the former England centre-half, recalls his days at Rotherham under Docherty. 'He believed in attacking the opposition whenever we had the ball. He used to tell us that the defenders were there to defend and no one would blame forwards for letting in goals. It was the job of forwards to attack and push for goals. His ideas on how we should approach the game led to attractive, attacking football. It was enjoyable playing his way and the lads liked it. It made us feel good.' Watson remembers the manager's attacking philosophy involved the team going forward as a unit with pace and keeping the ball moving. 'He had us in the best physical shape to achieve this and we used to swamp teams with sheer effort and movement.' Another diktat Docherty instilled into his players was to work harder than the opposition: 'You have ability,' he would say. 'Hard work will bring it out.'

Rotherham could often beat teams by sheer work-rate. 'Often teams couldn't keep up with us. He didn't like long-ball tactics, he liked us to attack together and keep the game flowing,' Watson recalls. There was also the attention to detail that Docherty demanded at free-kicks and dead-ball situations. 'He insisted we should mark players, not spaces. If the player you were supposed to be marking scored he played hell with you.'

Watson also felt the lash of Docherty's tongue during a club tour to Holland in the summer of 1968. In one game he was playing alongside the 40-year-old Docherty and made a defensive mistake: 'We brought you here to help us to win, not to lose the game for us,' he bawled at Watson.

'I resented his remarks at first because I didn't think the mistake was big enough to justify his outburst. I realised later it was part of his will to win.' Other players at Rotherham didn't always see eye to eye with their manager. 'There were personality clashes but most of the lads liked him and his philosophy.' And they liked his hard training sessions because they realised it would make them better players.

Docherty was a colourful character in more ways than one, remembers Watson: 'There was never a dull moment with Doc. He was brash and extrovert but if you trained hard, didn't shirk hard work and listened to what he had to say, you were all right with him and he treated you well.'

Tommy Cavanagh fully understood why the early influences had shaped Docherty's attacking beliefs. 'At Preston he played behind the greatest winger in the country, Tom Finney. He watched the maestro stretch defences and always believed you had to go out wide as a team to come in to the penalty area with maximum effect. He liked movement off the ball and a good passing game.' At Manchester United where he was his assistant coach, Cavanagh remembers he would shout to players in training to keep the ball moving. 'He made the game enjoyable for the lads and easy to play.'

Of Docherty as a manager and a man, the verdict of Cavanagh, who probably knew him as well as anyone, is worth recording. He rejects the suggestion that Docherty was self-destructive. 'He created enemies because he was a powerful man. He was the number one, the boss, and he let people know it. It's nonsense to think he had a chip on his shoulder because of his background in Glasgow. He had a forceful personality but there was a warm and generous side to him. Once it was the cleaning lady's birthday and he took her and her husband for an expensive meal. He was like that. It was a side of him people didn't always see. He wanted to be well thought of by people.

'His big thing was discipline. He would fall out with any player who tried to take advantage or broke the disciplinary code. He didn't like cheats and he told them so. That's why some people disliked him.' He also feels that Docherty made a rod for his own back with his outspokenness. 'He liked his name in the papers and often said the wrong things. He enjoyed being in the forefront. He wasn't afraid to make snap decisions and stand by them. He trod on toes, but his heart was in the right place. He had style and did nothing by half-measure. And he helped a lot of people on the way.'

Docherty plucked Dave Watson from Notts County for a bargain £1,000, plus Welsh international Keith Pring valued at £5,000, and took him to Rotherham. Watson had impressed Docherty while playing for Notts County reserves at Milmoor. When he went to collect his wages next day manager Billy Gray told him Docherty had made a bid for him.

'It came like a bolt out of the blue. I couldn't believe it.'

It was another example of Docherty's genius for spotting young talent. Watson, just 20, had been a professional for only eight months but went on to captain Manchester City and England as he established himself as one of the game's outstanding centre-halves. Watson remembers: 'He was very positive. I liked him straightaway. He told you what he believed in a no-nonsense way, and gave me a lot of confidence the first time I met him. People like him are few and far between. He was a tremendous motivator and able to make you believe in yourself. I really felt I could achieve anything on a football field under him.' At that time Newcastle manager Joe Harvey had been reported in the press as saying he didn't think Watson was good enough to make it at the highest level. 'It seemed to affect people's judgement of me, and I felt I might get left behind for honours. My game improved so much under Doc I was soon being tipped as a future England player. And he never let me down. If he promised anything he was as good as his word.'

Steve Coppell, still at university, was another young player spotted by Docherty and plucked from relative obscurity, this time third-division Tranmere Rovers. Twenty-four hours after signing him, Docherty named him in a full-scale practice game at Old Trafford. He was so impressed and certain he had an outstanding talent on his hands that he named him as substitute for the first-team game at Cardiff just four days later. And to boost the youngster's confidence even more he sent him on in the second half for Willie Morgan as United struggled. Coppell never looked back and went on to become an outstanding winger for England before injury cut short his playing career and he moved into successful management at Crystal Palace.

Willie Morgan had been in Scotland teams managed by Docherty and he actually recommended him for manager when asked by the Manchester United hierarchy. 'Docherty improvised and players wanted to play for him.

As a pure football manager he was the best. He knew footballers inside-out and I thought the world of him.'

At United the two men would fall out bitterly and end up facing each in court in a celebrated libel case which ended expensively for Docherty. And yet Morgan still admired him. 'He was brilliant at knowing how to blend a team. What I could never understand about him was why he had difficulties with people who thought the world of him. As far as football was concerned he was the best. In other matters off the field he left a lot to be desired.'

For most of the 1964–65 season Chelsea carried on from where they had left off, and by around the end of March 1965 everything looked very good indeed. They led the first division, they were firm favourites for the League Cup after beating Leicester 3–2 in the first leg of the final, and were also in the semi-finals of the FA Cup. An outrageous treble seemed there for the taking.

It started well as the League Cup was safely pocketed (0–0 in the second leg against Leicester) to guarantee the club's entry into Europe the following season. But perhaps it was the strains of ambition that caused the team to crack. First, they were beaten 0–2 by Liverpool in the FA Cup semi-final, and then they lost all form and slipped to third place in the league with Manchester United coming through to take the lead. Docherty was shattered. But there were still matches to play and it was his job to lift the youngsters for a last effort towards the remaining prize.

Included in the outstanding fixtures was a game against Burnely at Turf Moor, and according to Docherty's custom the team went first to Blackpool. He always took them there when they were playing in the north-west as he felt the sea air and the change recharged their batteries. This time the visit was to reverberate throughout the football world.

Docherty the disciplinarian could be tough and uncompromising in his pursuit of excellence on the field but he also had a fun-loving side and knew his young team needed time to relax. But they had to be treated like young adults, and that meant allowing them some freedom on trust. They were well paid to represent the club first and foremost, but no one minded anyone enjoying himself so long as it was kept within reason and not harmful to the club. There were unwritten rules which the players understood.

In the spring of 1965, however, the Chelsea players went over the top. When they did that Docherty acted swiftly and decisively and let the consequences take care of themselves.

I had let them go out on previous occasions and they had never let me down. It was important for them to be allowed to let their hair down on the trips away. I had no objections to a quiet drink in the evenings so long as they were back in the hotel at a reasonable time. I expected them to act like professionals. In Blackpool they let everyone down

– the fans, themselves, the club, and me. They also made a direct challenge to my authority. If I had ignored such a blatant breach of discipline I would have lost their respect anyway.

The night that shocked football started with Docherty's request to his players to be back in the hotel before midnight – preferably nearer eleven o'clock than twelve. Some of the players passed through the lounge to say good-night and then went out again via the fire escape. Docherty and some friends were in the lounge chatting over a quiet drink when the porter interrupted to complain that some of his players had been disturbing other guests. The porter also pointed out that the door to the fire escape had been opened: a serious breach of hotel rules because it affected the hotel's insurance. Confident that his lads would not be causing any trouble, Docherty asked the porter to get the master key so he could check the bedrooms. He checked several rooms and found them empty, and it slowly sank in that most of the team were still out on the town. He went back to the lounge and asked the porter to let him know the minute the players returned. He was in for a long wait. It was approaching four o'clock in the morning when the porter tipped him off that his players had crept back into the hotel up the fire escape. By now Docherty, having brooded about the blatant breach of discipline, was furious. He decided to confront his players and went back to check the rooms again.

The following minutes left the Chelsea manager even more incensed when the players tried to cover their tracks. He started with John Hollins and Barry Bridges, model professionals and usually well disciplined. Both players were in their separate beds, apparently asleep.

'Have you been sleeping all right, lads?' Docherty asked.

The players tried to bluff it out and did not respond. 'Did you hear me, lads?' Docherty pressed.

'Yes thanks, boss,' said one of them.

Docherty stepped forward and whipped away the bed-clothes: Hollins and Bridges were in bed both fully clothed as if they were ready to go out. It confirmed what the porter had said. Docherty left the two players under no illusions and told them they would be going back to London the next morning.

Next was Terry Venables. He was something of a ringleader and the younger players looked up to him. His room was empty but when Docherty rechecked later he found Venables had returned.

> He told me he had been in Eddie McCreadie's room all the time. I knew that was not true because I had already checked earlier and McCreadie's room was empty.

Docherty tried to get him to see sense and told him that it was no use covering up because the other lads had admitted they had come in late through the fire escape door.

> Venables still stuck to his story and I was getting very angry with him. I reminded him forcibly that we were

in Blackpool to prepare for a vital last effort in our Championship bid and not to mess around with no regard for the club and its fans. I told Terry I did not believe him and he would be going home with the others the next morning.

The next morning Docherty, who had finally got to his own bed around 4.30 a.m., called a meeting in the hotel lounge. Its purpose was to read the riot act before sending the culprits home in disgrace.

The high spirits of just a few hours earlier had now given way to a grim-faced group of Chelsea stars. For an hour the embarrassed footballers endured a verbal attack from the outraged manager. They listened uncomfortably as Docherty lectured them on how to behave as professionals and how they should conduct themselves when representing Chelsea. When he had finished he told the 'guilty eight' that they must be on the next train to London: the new captain, Terry Venables, George Graham and John Hollins, the three of them later to become managers in their own right of top clubs in the first division; the England centre-forward Barry Bridges, Eddie McCreadie, Bert Murray, Marvin Hinton and Joe Fascione.

Docherty never doubted for one minute that he was doing the right thing, but within hours he and his players were awash in stories of the biggest scandal to hit British football. The headline writers had a field day as Docherty was labelled variously 'a dictator', 'the headmaster' and 'sergeant-major'.

Once in London the players issued a statement saying

they had only had a bit of fun and had done nothing wrong, which did not help. And Terry Venables inflamed the situation further by talking to reporters.

Docherty's unswerving belief that discipline had to be enforced exacted its own heavy price. With eight first-team players missing, Chelsea lost 2–6 at Burnley, and their Championship dream ended in disillusionment and disappointment.

At the height of the affair Joe Mears had telephoned Docherty from abroad giving him full support for his actions:

> That was the tonic I needed because I knew there would be a lot of flak flying when I got back to London. It was a very welcome gesture from the chairman. But he was that sort of man. I could always count on his support.

Later, the 'guilty eight' were named in the team for the final match of the season against Blackpool at Bloomfield Road. Chelsea lost 2–3, in front of a 16,000 crowd, with a team which read as follows: Bonetti; Hinton, Ron Harris; Hollins, Mortimore, Upton; Murray, Graham, Bridges, Venables, Tambling. The goals were scored by Tambling and Mortimore.

It was a sad end to a season at one stage of which Chelsea had seemed to be in the running for no fewer than three major prizes. Even so, they had well and truly captured the imagination of the public. Over one million spectators had passed through Chelsea's turnstiles and the charisma of the sides they fielded, in their all-blue strip, and the brilliance of their play, would never be forgotten by those fortunate enough to watch them.

But at least Chelsea could now look forward to their first appearance in Europe, having qualified for the Inter-Cities Fairs Cup by winning the League Cup. Indeed, they were on the threshold of a tremendous season, with experience now added to their bubbling young talent.

6 Europe, and Double Trouble

After a summer tour of Australia and visits to Germany and Sweden, Chelsea reported back to the Bridge for the start of the new season in August 1965.

The mood was one of optimism. The team was full of skill; they had learned a lot from the previous season when the treble had slipped away so disappointingly, and they were generally more experienced. Docherty for one firmly believed they could go on and stamp themselves as the best team in the country. And best of all, they were to be in Europe for the first time.

For the then Inter-Cities Fairs Cup Docherty was leaving nothing to guesswork. He flew to Italy with his skipper Terry Venables to check on AC Roma who were coming to the Bridge. It would be an historic tie for Chelsea, but it would also make the headlines for its unacceptable face of player thuggery.

Docherty was to describe it as 'the most disgraceful affair' he had ever witnessed. Less than half an hour had gone when the Chelsea left-back Eddie McCreadie left the field in tears having been sent off for the first time in his career. He had been involved in a running battle with Leonardi, the Roma forward, being first kicked and cut brutally in the shin and then grabbed by the throat in separate clashes. Provoked beyond all patience, he retaliated and paid the ultimate penalty. Later he wrote to the chairman apologizing for 'letting the club down'.

In fact McCreadie's dismissal served only to stir Chelsea's determination. The ten remaining players responded in magnificent fashion and went on to a 4–1 victory with Terry Venables netting a dazzling hat-trick. It was all the sweeter for Docherty because even Venables had been subjected to what one newspaper described as the 'punching, butting and wild senseless kicking' of the Italians when he had to be carried from the pitch after being kicked in front of the referee.

It was a night Docherty remembered for something more than the supreme team effort, though. He had included the tall, thin, 19-year-old Peter Osgood in the team for only his second senior game, and the youngster strode through the rough-house with an elegant ease which stamped him as a future international.

Next day the press described 'this dreadful game' in these terms:

Inter-Cities Fairs Cup 1965–66
Chelsea 4 Roma 1
from The Times of September 23 1965

Chelsea took a comfortable lead over Roma in this first leg of their first round tie in the Inter-Cities Fairs Cup at Stamford Bridge last night, and from what my Italian colleagues tell me this should be more than enough for the return leg. Roma, they said, do not get off the floor like Inter-Milan.

At one time, as the first half developed, I felt there would be nothing but a police report or a dispatch from the battlefront when the game was over – casualty figures from each headquarters. The fact is that for almost three-quarters of an hour the match developed into nothing better than a Roman orgy, the roars for blood of the Stamford Bridge Coliseum in one's ears.

The football was about as moribund as a newly-landed trout, and the Italians clearly began the downfall with their close, niggling work. Chelsea, riled, retaliated in kind, and together they proceeded to kick the match half dead, rifle its pockets, and scatter the loot of a dreadful game into the night air.

The match had a real sense of tension and battle in the first half, with both sides searching mercilessly for the robes of power. By the interval, McCreadie had been sent off after an unseemly scuffle which ended with a perfect right hook to put Leonardi down for the count. Then Barison's name was taken, and Venables, the victim of the winger's vicious tackle, was carried from the field.

But already the Chelsea captain had scored twice through deceptively taken free-kicks, to which Barison had also replied with another free-kick to put Roma level at 1–1 by the 34th minute. Like the South Americans, Barison proved himself the master of the banana shot as he curled the ball, left-footed, over the line of Chelsea defenders past a surprised Bonetti.

As for Venables's two goals, the first came at the half hour when he shot Graham's flick through all eleven of Roma's team, compressed inside their own penalty area. The second, which gave Chelsea the lead, was nothing but a three-card trick. While Roma again built their wall inside their area, Venables pretended to mark out the paces from the ball, deceived the whole Italian team, took a neat flick from Bridges, and had infiltrated himself clear to shoot home.

But when Venables, on the stroke of half-time, was carried off and Chelsea reduced to nine men, we had had nothing to look forward to except some further bloodletting. But the unexpected happened, and a match that had built into a bonfire suddenly calmed to become a curious bundle of contradictions.

Within a minute of the restart, with Venables back to lead his side on to the field, he took a cross from Graham to volley a superb goal off the far post to put Chelsea more comfortably in the lead at 3–1. With 25 minutes left that became 4–1 when a glorious movement down the left between Fascione and Harris allowed Graham to nod in Harris's cross from the by-line.

From that moment all the bitterness went out of the game and Chelsea, already playing football, had finally persuaded the opposition to try to do the same. The Italians, though, were unable to match them, and it was Chelsea, stroking the ball around arrogantly, who saw the night out and themselves safe enough for the second leg in Rome on October 6.

Finally, something was rescued for football – by Venables,

the calm, complete commander-in-chief as he moved the pins on his map; by Harris, the dynamo, as he covered the whole left flank; and by Bridges, a firecracker in the forward areas.

Chelsea: Bonetti; Shellito, McCreadie; Hollins, Young, Harris; Bridges, Graham, Osgood, Venables, Fascione

Roma: Matteuci; Carponetti, Ardizzone; Carpanesi, Losi, Benaglia; Tomasini, Leonardi, Francesconi, Benitez, Barison

Having written to Docherty asking for a trial at the Bridge, Osgood had already demonstrated his talent the previous season when he illuminated his first-team debut against West Ham United and scored both goals in a 2–0 victory. The ball control and balance of this 'witty, likeable lad' made a tremendous and lasting impression on Docherty.

> He was such a deceptive player and made a big impact. I knew that night we had another world-class youngster on the books. Peter became a real crowd-pleaser and could lift the players around him with his inventive play. And he had a wonderful, easy-going temperament. To him football was to be enjoyed for what it essentially was . . . a game. A serious game, but a game just the same.

His influence on the team even so early in his career

could be judged when, in October 1966, he broke a leg in a League Cup-tie at Blackpool in a fifty-fifty tackle. Emlyn Hughes, the future England captain, challenged for the ball with Osgood, and the Chelsea man slumped to the floor writhing in pain. As Osgood was stretchered off everyone felt that his absence would badly damage the team's hopes for the season. It was a powerful blow to Docherty, who believed he had lost the final piece in a team jigsaw that would produce a picture of success.

Osgood had already been left out of the return leg of the Fairs Cup-tie in Rome, for Docherty wanted to nurse the youngster along and had decided that a 4-1 advantage could best be defended by his most experienced team, particularly as it looked like being another tough match – and this in front of a hostile crowd, too.

News had filtered through that the Italian press were conducting a hate campaign and using the McCreadie sending-off as their fuel to provoke animosity for Chelsea's visit. There was, too, a scurrilous claim that an Italian official had been abused: it was alleged that when he went into the Chelsea dressing-room to offer his congratulations he was told to get out or he would be thrown out. The hostility was brought into sharp focus the moment the Chelsea party arrived in Rome to find no Italian officials to greet them either at the airport or at the hotel. Docherty was incensed.

It was downright rudeness and a lack of basic courtesy that the Roma club did not see fit to have anyone there to greet us. They had been welcomed at Chelsea and were now showing us utter contempt. Everyone

– wives, players, directors – got the same ignorant treatment.

The inimical situation deteriorated as the team coach inched its way into the Flaminio Stadium for the game with an ugly crowd spitting and shouting abuse. When Joe Mears, as chairman of the FA, and his family and other Chelsea dignitaries walked onto the pitch they were bombarded with rotten fruit and any missile the crowd could throw at them.

Moreover, when the non-playing party went to their seats there was no escort. They were left to find their own way through the hostile, jeering fans; and then found they were not to be seated with the Roma officials in the directors' box but in a section some little way off.

It was an absolute disgrace, Joe Mears and his family being treated like that. It showed a total disrespect for his position. Joe Mears was a thorough gentleman and did not deserve such treatment. Yet the Italian police turned a blind eye. [When the players emerged from the tunnel they met an avalanche of missiles.] Everything was done to provoke my players and insult the club. There was not even a practice ball for them for the warm-up. They took the mickey out of the Italians by kicking around the rotten fruit that had been thrown at them. The intimidation was intense but I warned my players there must be no retaliation. How they kept their cool I'll never know. They were magnificent.

The atmosphere became even worse at the kick-off. Every time a Chelsea player touched the ball there was a cacophony of jeers and catcalls, and Peter Bonetti's goalmouth was littered with all manner of fruit. The first serious incident came when, in trying to punch clear, he inadvertently knocked down the Italian right-winger Tomborini and immediately the fruit was reinforced by a shower of bottles.

It was a marvel as the game went on that no one was hit whenever they were near the touchline or taking corners and throw-ins. Early in the second half, however, John Boyle, aged only 19 and a surprise choice at outside-left, was knocked unconscious when a bottle hit him on the head as he was taking a throw-in. It took the physio nearly five minutes to bring him round, whereupon with great courage the youngster insisted on still taking the throw despite having to once again turn his back to the screaming crowd. By a nice irony a tomato, meant for him, missed and sailed into the face of an Italian player – who in great anger then shook a fist at his own crowd!

Really serious injury was avoided only by inches when John Hollins had an iron stanchion, probably torn from a seat, thud into the turf at his feet. But Eddie McCreadie, for the home crowd the villain of the piece of course, was hit by another bottle and also knocked out. After that the spectators seemed to grow tired of the whole affair and even applauded some of the Chelsea moves as the game went on to a goalless draw so that the Londoners went through on a 4–1 aggregate.

Peter Bonetti had been receiving time signals from the bench and was slowly edging his way further out of goal to join the rest of the side as they ran for their lives at the final whistle. When someone pointed out to him in the dressing-room that he had left his gloves and a cap in the back of his net, he declined with some force any suggestion that he went back for them.

The players had answered Docherty's plea for restraint in the best possible fashion. But, with the crowd incensed that they had not succeeded in frightening Chelsea out of the match, he knew there was still danger ahead.

> We had to leave the stadium and I knew they would be waiting for us. They had one last go. Missiles started thudding into the side of the coach. We told the women to lie on the coach floor and the players put their bags and cushions up to the windows for more protection. But not before an iron bar smashed through one of the windows and showered glass fragments over everyone. That could have been fatal, and still the Italian police appeared disinterested. There was only a handful of policemen on duty and they did nothing to cool the situation. If my players had not shown such remarkable restraint throughout that trip there could have been a real tragedy on our hands. We were lucky to leave without casualties. I look back with admiration for my players. They were a credit to everyone. These were the same players I'd sent home in disgrace from Blackpool. They had wiped the slate clean with their magnificent conduct in Rome.

The atmosphere at the banquet that evening was distinctly chilly. When the Italian president spoke he made only a brief reference to the match; he apologised for the crowd's behaviour and added, 'I hope we meet again in a more pleasant atmosphere.'

Replying, Joe Mears made no reference to either the Roma club or the referee. He did, however, allow himself this comment: 'I make no apology for the words I am going to say. To the Chelsea team, you suffered the greatest provocation ever offered to any team. I have seen football all over the world and no side has ever had to suffer what you did tonight. And you did it with dignity and pride.'

Official recognition came with a message from Denis Howell, the minister with responsibility for sport, handed to Mr Mears when the party arrived back at London Airport the next day. It read, 'Please convey congratulations to the club and the team on their conduct and composure, which reflects great credit on British sport and themselves.'

As a result Roma were banned from Europe for three years. Docherty's verdict: 'They should have closed them down.'

Chelsea beat Weiner SK in the second round of the Fairs Cup and set their sights on a cup double in those heady days of spring 1966. First came an away third-round tie at first-division leaders Liverpool, the FA Cup holders, which seemed too big a hurdle to clear for Docherty's youngsters. Their hopes looked distinctly slimmer when with two minutes gone Liverpool scored through Roger Hunt. Enter the soaring talent of Peter Osgood, who equalised before half-time with a powerful header to give Docherty a platform for his interval pep talk. Midway through the second half Bobby Tambling clipped a second, and that proved to be Chelsea's winning goal.

Peter was such a match-winner and we had such all-round skill that they went out for the second half *believing* they would win. Liverpool were full of praise for our performance. They gave us the Cup and asked us to take it back to London to the FA headquarters. When we handed it in at Lancaster Gate we really believed it would be given back to us in May. We were that confident of winning it this time.

By now, though, the boat was being rocked. There were rumblings of discontent in the dressing-room, and Jim McCalliog and Barry Bridges wanted to leave. Docherty was also having something of a running argument with his outstanding full-back, Eddie McCreadie, Venables was giving trouble, and there were others involved in background disputes interwoven with success on the pitch.

There were those who thought that Docherty was reaping the seeds of resentment he had sown in Blackpool, but he took the view, 'The players do not have to like you but they must respect you and accept your decisions. You have to be the boss and stand by your decisions.'

Jim McCalliog was a bitter disappointment to Docherty, who had a high regard for his talent: 'I think he must have been approached by another club. I was very sorry to see him leave Chelsea. He was an exciting player and would have been a real asset.' Docherty was to get a further kick in the teeth after selling McCalliog to Sheffield Wednesday in October 1965 for £37,500, for it was the young Scot whose brilliant play for Sheffield Wednesday in the FA Cup semi-final that denied Chelsea an appearance at Wembley and took away one leg of the spectacular treble they had been chasing. Barry Bridges demanded his transfer after he was dropped just three days after playing at centre-forward for England against Austria at Wembley alongside Bobby Charlton and Jimmy Greaves. Docherty understood fully the damage to his pride and though he moved Bridges to the right wing to accommodate the burgeoning talent of Peter Osgood it was the beginning of the end of his time at Chelsea. Bridges left at the end of the season, joining Birmingham in a £55,000 move.

Eddie McCreadie was next into the manager's office demanding a transfer. He had been rowing with his manager on and off for eighteen months: 'We were a couple of fiery Scotsmen, although I felt he was the best full-back in the business.' McCreadie had been one of the eight players sent home from Blackpool and felt Docherty had mishandled the situation. Reserves Bert Murray and Joe Fascione, also two of the Blackpool eight, also wanted to leave and in January 1966 Docherty listed Peter Houseman and reserves Mick Jones, Jim Barron, Billy Sinclair and Jim Smart: 'I wanted players who would sweat blood for the Chelsea cause, and was always looking for better players than I had.' In April Docherty sacked his youth team boss Dick Foss after nineteen years at the club.

Meanwhile, always alert to the need for team-building, he continued to watch the transfer market closely for good players. A £70,000 bid for Arsenal centre-forward Joe Baker fell through, but it was essential to have a strong squad to cope with the extra demands of a congested fixture-list in the search for honours. The situation was highlighted when Chelsea were due to play the third round of the Fairs Cup against AC Milan just three days before the FA Cup fourth-round match against Leeds United.

Milan dominated the game in Italy but a George Graham goal in injury time gave Docherty real hope that his team could finish the job at the Bridge in the return leg. Their performance inspired Chelsea for the FA Cup-tie with Leeds which they won with the only goal of the game from Bobby Tambling to move into the fifth round and a clash with Shrewsbury. So far so good.

But the on-going success was putting more demands on the Chelsea youngsters. A 2–1 victory over AC Milan at the Bridge levelled the Fairs Cup tie at 3–3. Chelsea lost the toss in the boardroom for the choice of venue for the play-off and so it was back to Italy again. Amid heart-stopping drama they came through that game to round off a splendid spell for Chelsea, who had now beaten Liverpool and Leeds United to reach the fifth round of the FA Cup and had knocked out Roma, Weiner and mighty AC Milan in the Fairs competition. However, Docherty's determination to be the only boss in the dressing-room brought a long-running feud with his skipper Terry Venables to a head.

Venables had always set himself up as something of dressing-room spokesman. He started to challenge my authority in training. He would make sarcastic comments about what I was trying to put across. I would have welcomed constructive comments but Terry would tend to dismiss what I was saying. He wanted to be Mr Big in front of the lads, but what they didn't know was that he would often come to my office after training and apologise, saying he didn't mean any disrespect.

Just before the play-off against AC Milan in February 1966 Docherty acted swiftly to curb the disruptive influence of Venables and put him on the transfer list. 'This club's not big enough for the two of us,' he warned his 21-year-old skipper, who was also dropped from the team and told he would not be going to Milan. Docherty was willing even to put his own career on the line over the Venables issue, giving his chairman an ultimatum to back him or he would quit. Mears was saddened and had hoped it would not reach such an impasse but pledged his support for his manager, and Venables, a crowd idol at the Bridge, was put up for sale. A barrage of criticism rained down on Docherty but he countered by saying that constantly having his authority challenged was not acceptable: 'In any case Terry had been playing for himself, not the team.' To the press he responded defiantly: 'When I start worrying what people think of me I'll give up. It's my job to manage and do what I think is best for Chelsea Football Club.'

He was left in no doubt what Venables thought when Docherty was the only person on the staff at Chelsea not invited to the young man's wedding.

In Milan, Peter Osgood was given his chance to fill the role of Venables in the team and proved the wisdom of Docherty's thinking when he combined with George

Graham to set up a crucial goal for Barry Bridges to give Chelsea the lead. It was only in the closing seconds that Milan equalised through Fortunato – 'he was well named,' laughs Docherty now. It happened when three Chelsea players, confidently expecting a goal-kick, hovered and guarded the ball as it crossed the goal-line, but the referee awarded a corner. In the ensuing – and unwise – argument the Italians raced to take the kick which found the head of Fortunato and the defenders well out of position.

After thirty minutes of extra time the teams were still locked together and the players slumped to the turf in sheer exhaustion. The two captains now had to toss a coin to decide who would go through to the next round. Milan's Maldini and the Chelsea skipper Ron Harris watched nervously as the coin was flipped.

Standing at the side of the pitch Docherty knew the winner instantly as Harris threw his arms into the air in a gesture of delight. The young Chelsea team was through to the next European round against TSV Munich.

The Times recorded the events like this:

Inter-Cities Fairs Cup 1965–66
AC Milan 1 Chelsea 1
from The Times of March 3 1966

One can seldom come to the San Siro Stadium here and escape the Satanic undertones of drama. The steepling two-tiered stadium seems to be built for it. We certainly had almost everything tonight, a three-ringed circus as much as a football match, and at the end of it all it was Chelsea who survived a hectic night by the slender spin of a coin having drawn at four goals all with the famous Milan over three matches. They now come through to beat the Italians by the wheel of fortune after Maldini and his men had four times earlier in this competition for the Fairs Cup scraped through on a toss-up.

So Chelsea are now in the quarter-finals of the competition, and have not come to the end of their Continental road. They certainly grew up here tonight in a tense, tough atmosphere, with the baying of a 50,000 crowd in their ears. It might well have been the lions and Christians in the Colosseum of old.

But it was the last scene that lingered as the clock was creeping up towards midnight. Chelsea had taken the lead with a magnificent goal after only ten minutes; had held the advantage up to half-time, playing the game calmly off the cuff to master everything the Italians could offer.

Then the Italians, mounting their counter-challenge through the quickening pulse of the second half, equalized within seconds of the final whistle, when Fortunato headed in a corner from the right by Angellilo. Milan, indeed, were fortunate then, since Chelsea seemed justified in their strong protests, having let the ball run over the line for a goal-kick and finding themselves instead wrongly judged by a weak German referee.

And to add to it there, too, was Bonetti impeded as a swarm of players went up for the ball. Chelsea had been robbed and the stadium was a wild scene of excitement. But it was to come right in the end, dramatically. At the final whistle of extra time – two hours of hard slogging – several players collapsed with exhaustion. And, as bonfires were lit all round the stadium, Maldini, the Milan captain, had to wait some five minutes before Harris reappeared from the dressing-room to take part in the final decisive ceremony.

Nobody likes this way of deciding things, and one day surely the farce must be ended when so much is at stake. But there it was, and, as the multitude held its breath and a coin spun in the air from the referee's hand, there suddenly was the figure of Harris leaping for joy to tell the world the answer.

So the pipe dream came true after all and there was a ring of truth about it when one remembers the way Chelsea had played over the first hour on a night when the city of Milan had a foot in two worlds – Internationale far away in Budapest as they moved into the semi-final of the European Cup, AC Milan here, who are now left behind in the shadows.

It was not a great match, but it had its character, and it was a great effort by Chelsea against a side of undoubted artists. But it was a Milan side without talented Rivera and Schnellinger, the great German full back – both injured in Naples on Sunday – and without Amarildo, the Brazilian World Cup player, who had been dropped from the side. But it showed the depths of the Italian reserves.

Chelsea, too, were without Venables, for whom Murray deputized as the midfield worker and, though no great intellectual, produced a high work rate in midfield in support of the elegant Osgood. So on one side we had the pattern-weaving artistry and the feathery touch of Milan, and on the other the high mobility and the overlapping runs of Chelsea as backs and half-backs used the width of the field down the flanks.

So these varying rhythms worked themselves out and as the night unwound Chelsea paced their game cleverly, husbanding their resources and playing it cool, always calm and collected and slowing down the game to their own tempo. And as the night grew on, Milan grew desperate as they tried to break down the clever covering work of a fine Chelsea defence, in which Hinton, as usual, played magnificently in his quiet, unobtrusive way and Harris, too, was a young lion.

The Chelsea goal so soon after the start shook the Milanese. It was begun by Osgood in midfield. He put his foot on the ball, played for time, changed direction twice, flicked a perfect pass diagonally to Graham. There followed an instantaneous wall pass from the inside right through the Italian defence and there was Bridges at centre-forward to flash in a perfect low shot left footed.

It was a knife straight under the Milan ribs, and an Italian colleague near by could only turn and say expressively: 'Bellissimo, bellissimo.' There Chelsea stayed till half-time as the referee more and more found himself jostling players and the crowd more and more bayed for blood.

Twice in the opening quarter of an hour of the second half Chelsea all but added to their lead. Once a quick move between Osgood, Graham and Boyle saw the ball flash across an unguarded goal with no one able to supply the last delicate touch. Then Bridges broke free down the left from a long pass by McCreadie. With Graham running in at his side again in front of an unguarded goal he pulled his pass behind his colleague and another fleeting chance had gone.

It was now over the last half-hour of normal that the Italians began to raise their steam. Shots by Angelillo, Madde and Sormani almost hit the bull's-eye. But Bonetti was in fearless mood, showing what a fine pair of hands he has. With only two minutes left he made a flying, prehensile save from an overhead bicycle shot from the talented Sormani.

Then with only seconds left came that doubtful corner-kick, Fortunato's header to bring the scores level again. The stadium exploded. Cushions rained down like leaves and after a short breather they were at it again. Now it is all over. The Italian bonfires are out, but Chelsea are in.

Milan: Balzarini; Pelagilli, Trebbi; Santin, Maldini, Grossetti; Lodetti, Madde, Sormani, Angelillo, Fortunato

Chelsea: Bonetti; Ron Harris, McCreadie; Hollins, Hinton, Boyle; Bridges, Graham, Osgood, Murray,

The important match now was the FA Cup-tie with Shrewsbury. Venables was recalled for the injured John Hollins. Docherty said defiantly at the time, 'He's a Chelsea player and will play for the club if I need him in the team. When I dropped him against Milan in the play-off I did not say he would not play for Chelsea again. He's back in the team again but he's still up for sale.' The bandwagon was still rolling, with a 3–2 victory over Shrewsbury and a sixth-round tie with Hull City.

Docherty moved again into the transfer market, signing Joe Kirkup from West Ham United before flying off to Germany to check out TSV Munich. At the airport Docherty heard that Manchester United were arriving from Spain where they had beaten Benfica 5–1 in the European Cup; he waited to congratulate Matt Busby and George Best who had scored a brilliant goal. The next day, with Docherty still in Germany, Chelsea beat United 2–0 at the Bridge. The new signing, Joe Kirkup, kept Best quiet and the transfer-listed Venables turned in a man-of-the-match performance for the crowd of over 60,000.

The following week, with the pace really hotting up, Chelsea flew into Munich in a blizzard. Docherty named the team that had humbled Manchester United the previous Saturday, and in treacherous conditions with a carpet of snow covering the pitch they drew 2–2. When they arrived back in London Docherty took Venables off the transfer list.

Surprisingly Chelsea could only draw with Hull in the FA Cup which meant two vital games the following week at the Bridge: the return tie with Munich and the replay with Hull. Two vital games in three days, and with Osgood in bed ill over the weekend, Docherty began to doubt the wisdom of not asking for the FA Cup replay to be put back to a later date. The young star recovered in time for Tuesday's leg with Munich, however, and again proved his value. He scored a superb winner to take Chelsea through to the Fairs Cup semi-finals even though he was tiring fast towards the end. He was ordered straight back to bed so that he would be rested before Thursday's replay against Hull.

Chelsea took a 2–0 lead over Hull only to see the visitors cut the deficit. Again it was Osgood with a deceptive run who set up the third and decisive goal for Bobby Tambling to score. Now they had to face mighty Barcelona in the semi-final of the Fairs Cup . . . just three days before the FA Cup semi-final against Sheffield Wednesday at Villa Park. Stamford Bridge was buzzing with the mouthwatering prospect of the club's first cup double, which would erase the disappointments of the previous season.

When Docherty arrived at Stamford Bridge on the morning of the European tie the pitch was flooded from days of heavy rain, and the game was called off after a referee's inspection in mid-afternoon. The Spaniards were furious and their coach insisted the pitch was fit enough to play on. Docherty reacted with some vigour.

I told him the pitch was badly cut up because he had insisted on his players training on it the night before. Then we had Tambling and McCreadie injured, but Barcelona believed I had influenced the ref because they were unable to play and because we had the FA Cup semi three days later. It was nonsense, of course, but the Spaniards wouldn't listen. They even accused

me of deliberately watering the pitch. That would have
been pointless because it was already flooded.

Chelsea's momentum drained away in the rain, and they
lost in the FA Cup semi-final, beaten 2–0 by Sheffield
Wednesday. Villa Park was muddy and the surface heavy.
It took away the extra skills of the Chelsea youngsters
who were also up against a hard-tackling Wednesday
defence. A week that had started on a high note had
ended miserably. Docherty did his best to console his
shattered team, out of the Cup at the semi-final stage for
the second year running. They had to get over it quickly
with the other semi coming up against Barcelona. After
the abandoned game at the Bridge, this had been made
the first leg, with the second back in London.

Meanwhile the dressing-room unrest continued and
Docherty was hunting new men. Now he flew to Scotland;
his target Dundee's inside-forward Charlie Cooke. He
wasted no time. The deal was completed over breakfast
at the Royal Caledonian Hotel in Edinburgh the next
morning, and forty-eight hours later Cooke was in the
Chelsea party that flew to Barcelona.

There was another worry. Defeat in the FA Cup semis
was accompanied, not unsurprisingly, by a dip in League
form as the team slipped out of the top three in the first
division so that if Chelsea wanted to stay in Europe the
following season they *had* to win the Fairs Cup. It would
be a truly tremendous performance if his youngsters could
pull it off. But the rub of the green was going against
Docherty, as George Graham joined Eddie McCreadie on

the injured list and Cooke failed a fitness test with a calf injury and could not play against Barcelona. Neither did Venables help by insisting that Cooke had been bought as his replacement. He was told there was room for him and Cooke in the team, but he clearly did not like it. With Venables by now smarting on several fronts, and with Tottenham Hotspur showing an interest, it was clearly only a matter of time before player and manager would part company.

Barcelona won the Fairs semi 2–0 with Venables and Hollins kicked viciously and needing treatment, although Barcelona players tried to haul them up off the pitch because they thought they were feigning injury.

Afterwards, Docherty told Venables that he would not play for Chelsea again. It was academic anyway. When Chelsea flew back to London Spurs were waiting with an offer of £70,000 for him. Docherty sent a message to the Spurs manager Bill Nicholson that they valued Venables at £10,000 more and the deal was settled.

Despite all these problems Chelsea responded magnificently to pull back the two-goal deficit against Barcelona at the Bridge, winning 2–0 to level the Fairs Cup semi-final on aggregate. But they lost the toss for choice of venue and had to return to Spain for the deciding match.

After congratulating his players in the dressing-room on their win Docherty left for the boardroom for a celebration drink. He was in for a nasty surprise, and within minutes he was threatening to quit.

This time the trouble came from a totally unexpected

quarter: Peter Bonetti and Bobby Tambling, part of England's 1966 World Cup squad, and two of his most loyal players, wanted to leave. Both had refused new contracts and a pay rise offered to all the first-team players as a thank-you from the board for the season's efforts. Not only had the team reached the FA and Fairs Cup semi-finals but they had sharply increased revenue at the turnstiles and had also performed well in the League, finishing in fifth place. Chairman Mears had met both players after the Barcelona game to try to find out why they were unhappy. When Mears told Docherty he had agreed an extra £10,000 for each player, to be spread over the period of their new contracts, Docherty decided it was time to go himself.

> I couldn't believe my ears. I felt let down by the chairman for the first time since I had joined the club. I could not believe he had gone behind my back and given in to the players. There were other players who had accepted new terms without anything extra and who were just as loyal to the club. I didn't mind if all the players were to be given an extra £10,000, but not just the two of them.

Docherty told Mears, 'Some players say they would like to leave because they don't like me. Will you give them big pay-outs to keep them as well?' There was an awkward silence between the two men. Solemnly Mears pointed out that the two players had also complained of being away from their families too often. Furiously Docherty defended: 'I do not keep them away from home deliberately. If we are successful we have to travel. If they don't like it they should get a job in an office or find a club that does not win things. You gave me full control over the playing side. If you agree to their demands then I must leave the club.'

Another awkward silence followed before Mears told Docherty he was right, and apologised for interfering.

> Joe Mears was a very fair-minded chairman and obviously thought he was doing right for the club. What a superb man. For a chairman to admit he was wrong was incredible. It would be unthinkable in today's football. But if he had given in then the players would have ruled me. Bonetti and Tambling were refused their £10,000. That was the right course of action. They were a long way from the bread queue on their wages, I can assure you.

Both players signed new contracts, although Docherty sensed they were 'a bit sour' in their attitude towards him for a time, and indeed Bonetti was to write later in a newspaper that his manager made him 'sick to the teeth'. The article also accused Docherty of broken promises over bonuses and treating players one minute like kings and the next like dirt. It was strong stuff, yet Docherty didn't try to prevent publication of the article.

The incident served to warn Docherty that the situation could crop up again and he acted accordingly. As the team prepared for its flight to Barcelona for the Fairs Cup semi-final decider he moved swiftly for Millwall's Alex Stepney, backing his judgement with a then world record offer for a goalkeeper of £50,000. Stepney signed in time to fly out with his new team-mates, although Docherty kept Bonetti in the team. He now had two world-class goalkeepers, but he wanted to be sure his players wanted to play for Chelsea. In the event Bonetti stayed and it was Stepney who moved, to Old Trafford, just 112 days, five pre-season matches, two reserve-team games and one first-team League appearance after signing. At least he had the consolation of Docherty saying that he had found himself with 'the two best goalkeepers in the country'.

In Barcelona, Chelsea's young team suffered the consequences of too many matches and disappointments that season as they slumped to a heavy defeat by 0–5.

We were well beaten by Barcelona but the stuffing had been knocked out of my lads in the FA Cup semi-final defeat by Sheffield Wednesday. They had not really recovered from that. They were in terrific form and going so well before coming unstuck in the mud at Villa Park. I remember a lot of tearful young lads in the dressing-room after that game. They had gone out that afternoon really believing Wembley was waiting for them. It was the first major disappointment for many of them because they were still learning. My heart went out to them. I deeply felt their sense of disappointment.

7 Brighton and Bermuda

The summer of 1966 dealt Docherty a grievous personal blow when Joe Mears, the man who had given him his first chance in football management, collapsed and died outside an Oslo hotel where he'd been staying while on business. Things at Chelsea were never to be the same again for him. 'I thought I was at Chelsea for life. I had a truly magnificient chairman in Joe Mears. He was a marvellous man to work with and understood how I wanted to do things and always gave me support and advice. I never really felt as happy or comfortable again once he had gone.' The truth was that he didn't really get on with Mears's successor Charles Pratt. 'We didn't see eye to eye on lots of things, and I knew then that it would not work out for me any more.'

England's World Cup triumph that summer had inspired and thrilled the domestic game. The victorious echoes of the memorable win over West Germany at Wembley were still ringing in the ears of football fans throughout the land when the new season started in August. But Docherty believed that the England boss Alf Ramsey had ignored most of the available talent at the Bridge and he pledged to himself that the coming season would prove his point.

His team had been in the top five of the first division for three consecutive seasons. Their highest position was third in 1965 when victory in the Football League Cup final had qualified them for Europe, and although they faded the experience had given the emerging Chelsea youngsters the know-how to back their natural skills. Docherty was convinced it would give them the vital ingredient to be champions and gain further honours. It might have been Chelsea's year, as Docherty had hoped, until the tragic accident to Osgood when he broke his leg at Blackpool.

The season was also to be stained by an unsavoury row over the allocation of tickets for a cup-tie at Brighton which had repercussions even when Chelsea reached the first-ever all-cockney Cup final, against Tottenham Hotspur.

Docherty's first inkling of unrest came after a game against Manchester City at the Bridge. The players were angry about their allocation of tickets for the FA Cup fourth-round tie at Brighton the following week. Docherty sympathised but pointed out it was away from home and there would be fewer tickets to go round the club: he told them not to get steamed up about it and promised to talk to the secretary, John Battersby, and see what could be done.

The meeting with Battersby only served to exacerbate the issue. He pointed out that the allocation for the players would be two complimentary tickets, along with ten seat tickets and ten more in the standing areas which they could buy.

Battersby then made a silly statement. He told me the allocation would be the same if the team got to Wembley. It was only the fourth round coming up. It was ridiculous to be making statements about Wembley. That should surely be a board matter, anyway. The players were already upset about the allocation for Brighton the following week. If I had told them it would be the same if they had the good fortune to go all the way to Wembley, you can imagine what their reaction might have been. But even at that early stage I could see it was going to be a problem. The club's attitude was a nonsense whichever way you looked at it. But with the chairman Charles Pratt there were no shades of opinion, and Battersby was just the board's mouthpiece.

Some of the Chelsea players lived in the Brighton area and Docherty felt that perhaps a special case could be pleaded on their behalf.

They could surely have been given an extra couple of tickets. It annoyed me when the chairman told me he had no intention of defending his decision with the players and flatly refused my request to have a quiet chat with them. All that before an important cup-tie. Joe Mears would have sorted it out with no trouble.

The situation deteriorated when the players felt they were being accused of being greedy. The suggestion was that they wanted extra tickets to sell on the black market to make extra cash. Once they had that idea the situation got out of control. Docherty was now embroiled in a full-scale row, with himself in the middle between the players on one side and the board on the other.

The squabbling was no good for the team or the club and was handled badly at board level. It was something Joe Mears would not have allowed to happen. But then I told his successor Charles Pratt that he had worked with Joe for twenty-five years and had learned nothing.

The fence was never a place on which Docherty could sit, and with predictable boldness he backed his players and made his own grand gesture by giving his directors' box ticket next to the chairman to a friend for the tie at Brighton. His stand against his bosses incurred a predictable wrath and he got a telephone call at his Brighton hotel to attend the board meeting the following Wednesday at Stamford Bridge – which, as it happened, would be the day of the replay, after a draw at Brighton.

Docherty's instinctive reaction was that it must be serious. A journalist friend confirmed it when he tipped him off that he was going to be carpeted. Apparently the directors had been outraged by his public outburst over the ticket allocation for the Cup-tie at Brighton. They were linking this latest incident to newspaper articles he had also written which had pulled no punches about the club. Whatever the rights and wrongs of the situation the timing of the Chelsea board meeting left Docherty totally exasperated. His team was playing in a crucial tie that night, and instead of leaving him to get on with that the directors wanted him at a meeting to give him a telling-off. Or maybe worse. He had just signed a new five-year contract until 1972 but he could have been accused of breaking the terms by disagreeing publicly with the directors, especially with the chairman Charles Pratt. He more than half expected the sack.

In the boardroom Docherty predictably was accused over his public outbursts against the board and his controversial views about the club on radio, television and in the press. The most serious accusation was that he had insulted the chairman by giving away his ticket in the directors' box. There was a logic about the situation that Docherty was forced to concede despite his pride; he could not lambast his directors in public if he in turn wanted their backing in enforcing discipline with his players.

> They were absolutely right on that point, but I told them I had backed the players because the directors had not acted to prevent the situation arising. It was *their* job to sort things out before they got out of hand. They had provoked the row themselves with their attitude of take-it-or-leave-it.

He defended himself without too much conviction, realising that if the board wanted to they could end his contract there and then. He was asked to leave the room while the directors discussed his position. Twenty-five minutes later he was summoned again and told forcefully that they considered him out of order. Warned as to his future conduct and reprimanded, Docherty left fuming.

> I had a cup-tie to win that night and here I was being told off by the very people who should have at least let me get on with the job in hand before having a go at me. But it was that kind of stupidity that had brought the whole nonsense about in the first place.

Back in the dressing-room he did not mention the incident during his team talk, and his young players flowed to an emphatic 4–0 victory to move effortlessly into the FA Cup fifth round.

Next morning the game took second place as the front pages splashed the story of Docherty's confrontation in the Chelsea boardroom and its outcome.

> I felt like quitting there and then. I had built up the
> Chelsea team from a music-hall joke to one that
> was admired throughout football, and now this. But
> I asked myself why should I walk out on the years
> of hard work because the directors had belittled me
> publicly? I decided to stay despite them.

Peace was restored and Docherty's team would go on to challenge for more honours, though it would not be long before he would once again swim in troubled waters.

A fifth-round victory over Sheffield United set up a revenge match over Sheffield Wednesday in the next round of the FA Cup. Wednesday had started Chelsea's slide the previous season when they won the semi-final at Villa Park; but Chelsea made no mistake this time to reach their third semi-final in consecutive years with a Tommy Baldwin goal in injury time for a 1–0 victory.

And so Chelsea had to overcome Leeds United if they wanted to reach Wembley. After recent years they were in a very determined mood. They struggled against injuries in the build-up and team planning was difficult. Three key players, Tony Hateley, Charlie Cooke and John Boyle, were under intensive treatment for injuries and Eddie McCreadie had also been out and was doubtful. They all won their battle for fitness, and it was Tony Hateley, 'the best header of a ball in Europe', who put Chelsea in front just before half-time. Leeds thought they had equalised in injury time when a Peter Lorimer free-kick crashed into the Chelsea net but it was disallowed by referee Ken Burns, who ruled that he had not blown the whistle for the kick to be taken.

And so, by the only goal, Docherty and his young team reached Wembley at last. Their opponents would be Tottenham Hotspur.

The row over the Brighton ticket allocation would not go away. The club had thrown a heavy pebble in the water at the time by insisting that if the team reached the final the allocation would be the same: ten tickets to buy and two complimentaries. Now the ripples were being felt as Docherty was having to tell the players the same story while trying to concentrate their thoughts on the game. Incredibly the directors inflamed the situation further when they let it be known on the eve of the final that the players would get only £50 appearance money unless they won the Cup, in which case they would share a kitty of £12,000. The effect on young men whose skills had got the club to Wembley in the first place and had brought cash flowing into the bank can well be imagined, especially when they found out that Spurs were paying their team a substantial bonus win or lose.

They agreed to keep quiet but decided they would

demonstrate their anger by boycotting the club's official banquet at the Carlton Tower Hotel. Docherty pleaded with them not to carry out the threat, warning them it would almost certainly lead to the cancellation of the summer tour to the United States and Bermuda, something they deserved after their hard work. It was a plea that would come back to haunt him.

It was an all-London final and Chelsea's first for some fifty years, so the atmosphere that May afternoon was unusual even for Wembley. Spice was added by the fact that in the Spurs line-up were Terry Venables and the goal machine Jimmy Greaves, both former Chelsea favourites. Even so, Docherty's team had a distinct look of quality about it: Peter Bonetti, 'The Cat', in goal; Alan Harris, Eddie McCreadie; John Hollins, Marvin Hinton, Ron Harris; Charlie Cooke, Tommy Baldwin, Tony Hateley, Bobby Tambling and John Boyle.

Opposing them were Jennings; Kinnear and Knowles; Mullery, England, Mackay; Robertson, Greaves, Gilzean, Venables, Saul.

The match proved to be another so-near-yet-so-far Wembley visit for Docherty. The worst time to concede a goal in a tight match is just before half-time, and this is just what Chelsea did – when, with a little luck, they might easily have been in the lead. Docherty maintains that towards the end of the game Tottenham were struggling, but his own side's goal came too late to influence the result.

Things began to go wrong for Chelsea in the sixth minute when McCreadie tore his shoulder ligaments stretching to head a shot clear. It was not all gloom and doom, however. Bonetti had a great game in goal, Ron Harris completely neutralised Greaves, whilst the five shots that Hollins had at goal were among the best to be seen. On the other hand, Tambling's impact was much less than usual.

In fact, Chelsea might very easily have taken the lead literally seconds before Spurs scored the first goal of the match. Cooke, weaving in from the right, fired in a shot that was heading straight for the far corner of the net before Jennings just managed to touch it over the bar. From the corner, however, Mullery got the ball, surged downfield and found his shot cannoning back off Ron Harris's leg. It ran sweetly for Robertson, whose volley gave Bonetti no chance. One down at half-time, they came out again and almost immediately missed equalising when Tambling got a foot to a wonder pass across the goalmouth from Alan Harris only to see the ball go wide by the proverbial width of a bootlace.

Twenty minutes into the second half Frank Saul scored again, and no one could deny the element of luck in it. He found the ball running loose towards him, and as he confessed later he turned and belted it without the slightest idea where it was going. Its destination turned out to be the corner of the net farthest from Bonetti. Eventually Tambling headed one past Jennings, but by then there were only four minutes of the game left. Even so, in the dying seconds Hollins made a final, despairing effort to salvage at least a draw; but 2–1 it remained.

At the banquet after the game, Docherty could not

restrain himself when club officials gave their speeches: 'Ladies and gentlemen, I am glad to mention the people who seem to have been forgotten. I'm referring, of course, to the people who got us here . . . my players. I am proud of them.' The comment was just another ingredient in the potent cocktail that was poisoning Docherty's position, along with the rows; the confrontation with his directors over the ticket allocations; the newspaper articles he had written; a £100 fine for calling a referee a 'bloody disgrace' after the Chelsea youth team had played Queen's Park Rangers and had three penalties awarded against them ('To award three penalties against kids *was* a bloody disgrace'), and his fiery, outspoken manner. The final item in the recipe was not long delayed, and was found in – of all unlikely places – Bermuda.

During their summer tour, begun just thirty-six hours after the Cup final the team were playing a Bermuda XI in a so-called friendly and leading 7–0. The game was in its last couple of minutes when the local referee sent off Tony Hateley and Barry Lloyd, whereupon Docherty jumped up and asked why.

'Get off the pitch, white man,' was the response.

'What did you say?' asked Docherty. The words were repeated. 'You should be swinging from a tree, not refereeing,' Docherty snapped back in ill-judged, heat-of-the-moment anger.

In England some weeks later the referee's report brought swift and crushing retribution from the FA: a month's suspension from football anywhere in the country, the financial blow of losing his wages, and the harsh reality that his ban meant he could not even enter his own office at Stamford Bridge. Overnight Docherty had been branded an outcast, and without even being asked his side of the story – convicted, as he puts it, without a trial.

Diplomacy had never been his strong point. Now the Bermuda incident was the last straw with the club.

Things had never been the same for me under the chairmanship of Charles Pratt. We had a mutual understanding . . . we disliked each other.

In October 1967 the isolated Docherty handed in his resignation to the board. Chairman Pratt accepted it. His break with the Bridge was final.

8 On the Move

In contrast to high-powered Chelsea, Tommy Docherty's next move, to a Rotherham United well ensconced in the bottom half of the second division, was not all gold and glitter. Unlike the London scene it was a club with a family atmosphere, but it was a family fallen on hard times and grimly expecting no improvements. The quiet, reserved chairman, Eric Purshouse, felt Docherty could bring some hope and sparkle to the club, and brought him back up north.

> I liked the facilities. The players were a good bunch who didn't think of themselves as big-timers, and the people running the club, from the chairman down, were friendly and easy to deal with. I was very impressed with the chairman. He told me he knew nothing about football so he gave me complete control. I realised he was special when he said I could sell the ground if I thought it would help Rotherham United Football Club. I made a promise to him that I would take the club out of the second division. I did. I took it straight into the third.

He was still headline news having left Chelsea a month earlier in a blaze of publicity following his sensational resignation, but Purshouse admired the volatile, out-spoken Scot and felt he was just the man to revive the flagging fortunes of his struggling club.

Docherty arrived at Rotherham like a whirlwind blowing through Millmoor and shaking the place to its foundations before leaving just as quickly a year later. He stamped his authority all over the place, clearing out the old, introducing young players into the first-team squad, pruning, buying and selling in a pattern similar to the one he had established at Chelsea as he rebuilt a team to prepare for the immediate job of fighting against relegation. The whole town responded, with home gates up an average of 5,000 and Docherty the talk of pubs and clubs across Yorkshire.

He realised very quickly that the team was simply not good enough. Two defeats in his first three games in charge gave him a sharp reminder of the difficulties that lay ahead. He acted swiftly in characteristic fashion. Four players were dropped and four others transfer-listed. He advised the directors that the playing staff of twenty-seven professionals needed cutting by at least half a dozen. The local press latched on to his mood, describing him as a 'friendly hurricane'. Unperturbed, he set about demolishing the team and rebuilding it just as quickly, demonstrating his talent for spotting young players of potential by plucking Dave Watson from Notts County reserves, a move which would make the club a handsome profit when Watson was eventually sold for a six-figure fee to Sunderland.

The team became harder to beat, but the fight against

112

relegation was not just in the hands of Docherty, for survival depended also on results elsewhere among the other struggling clubs. As the season reached its climax he was encouraged by a splendid 2–0 victory at Bolton Wanderers and a single-goal victory at home over fellow strugglers Plymouth Argyle. But, despite the end-of-season flourish, Rotherham slipped into the third division. Docherty decided it was time to reorganise the non-playing side of the club to prepare for the different challenge that lay ahead in the lower division.

Mindful that some decisions would be hard to take and unpopular he pressed ahead, deciding it was in the club's best interest if he sacked the physiotherapist Bernard Grimmer and groundsman Eric Scott, men who had been with the club a number of years. He then made the head trainer Albert Wilson the groundsman, insisting that three men had been doing the work of two. The moves earned him a reputation of being ruthless but he hit back.

> I drive myself as hard as the players or anyone else at the club. I look for dedication and hard work and make decisions for the club and its future well-being.

There were pluses, of course, as the team reached the fifth round of the FA Cup for the first time in its history and netted a handsome profit of £25,000, and there was the extra revenue created by the increased gates. The gains were short-term from his point of view and, inevitably, when he answered a call from Queen's Park Rangers he was under fire from people who felt that he had merely used Rotherham as a stepping-stone.

It was not true, of course. I was very happy indeed at the club and had full control and the backing of a marvellous chairman, but Queen's Park Rangers were in the first division and it seemed a challenge I could not refuse.

His departure after a little over one year was accompanied by the unflattering echo from disappointed supporters that he was the 'big-time gamble that had failed.' Chairman Purshouse was more magnanimous, releasing him from his contract without a demand for compensation and with his blessing. The less charitable people at the club felt he had left them in debt and in the third division.

Some people claim that I left Rotherham in debt. That was untrue. Dave Watson was just one example. I bought him for peanuts and Rotherham sold him for £100,000. We also made a good few bob by reaching the fifth round of the FA Cup. I had a thoroughly enjoyable time at Rotherham, and Eric Purshouse was smashing to work with. How many club chairmen would take the players and manager for a sunshine holiday in Spain? That's what the board did for us after we were relegated, and Mr Purshouse picked up the bill.

Of Queen's Park Rangers Docherty says now, 'The

challenge was fine, the move disastrous. I walked after a month.'

The chairman, Jim Gregory, wielded absolute power at Loftus Road.

He was a man of power and moods. He owned the club and obviously we had to agree with any decision that was made, otherwise he would enforce the veto. Jim had many excellent qualities which I liked and was very decisive if he agreed with you. But he was temperamental to work with at other times. I soon realised it was not going to work out between us. I like to be my own man and make my own decisions. We were too much alike, and it became apparent very quickly that I had made the wrong move from Rotherham. Jim had the club's best interests at heart and so did I, but we just saw things differently. Jim explained what powers I would have in thirty seconds: none. It took me another fifteen seconds to realise I had to go.

Docherty tried to go through the motions, hoping he had misjudged the position, and soon after his arrival he was making a bid to sign his first player. He tried to contact Gregory but he was on a health farm. When he eventually got him to the telephone the conversation was short and sharp.

'Jim, I would like to buy Brian Tiler from Rotherham.'

'How much?'

'£100,000.'

'I don't agree.'

'Chairman, it isn't going to work between us. I'm leaving.'

'What?'

'I'm quitting.'

'You're joking.'

'It doesn't sound funny from where I am. I'll be packing my bags in the morning.'

And so, twenty-eight days after leaving Rotherham, Docherty was leaving QPR, the shortest managerial reign of even his much-travelled career. But Jim Gregory must have liked something about his style, for ten years later he was on the telephone again asking him to give it one more try.

Immediately after leaving Loftus Road, a tip-off from a friend sent him heading for Gatwick airport and the next flight to Spain, where Atletico Bilbao wanted a coach. Docherty's fame had gone before him, and he shook hands on a deal, intending to sign the contract when he returned to take charge of the team. However, the move was dramatically called off when the Bilbao president was killed in a car crash shortly after offering the job to Docherty.

Next, a telephone call from another friend from his Chelsea days turned his attentions to second-division Aston Villa: a London bank official, Pat Mathews, who had been monitoring the club's share situation, wanted to speak with Docherty. The two men met. The club was in turmoil with a power struggle going on in the boardroom, but Docherty learned that a Birmingham director, Doug Ellis, might become the next Villa chairman. Quickly they worked out a three-year deal for Docherty to manage the club when the boardroom situation was sorted out. Within hours Docherty was talking with Doug Ellis. They started as they parted thirteen months later . . . with a difference of opinion. Ellis told him he did not think they could afford his wage demands; Docherty told him he should wait until he was chairman before deciding.

After a short while, in December 1968, a new board was formed at Villa Park with Ellis as chairman and Docherty in the manager's seat just three weeks after he had quit Queen's Park Rangers. He was to find Villa his toughest job in management. The team was having a miserable time and unable to get the results to lift the gloom. Moreover, although the fans had welcomed the brash, outspoken Docherty with a belief that he would breathe fire into the club, they turned on him when things started to go wrong, calling him Dr Dolittle.

Villa escaped relegation, but started the 1969–70 season disastrously: 'Blame me, not the board; I am the manager,' Docherty told the fans defiantly as the team settled on the bottom of the second division.

> Doug Ellis told me not worry, the board was a hundred
> per cent behind me. I told him I wanted him in front
> of me so I could see what he was up to.

One point from the first five matches, though, and Docherty's head was on the chopping block. He brought in a new assistant, Vic Crowe, who eventually replaced him, but the team continued to struggle and although Docherty offered to work without pay to prove he could bring better results the board pressed the panic button early in 1970. A crisis meeting was called and Docherty asked to be there. The meeting lasted over seven hours and he was kept waiting ignominiously outside.

> Doug Ellis finally emerged from the meeting and told me, 'Tommy, we've given you a vote of confidence.' I said, 'Thanks, chairman. I'll pack my bags and clear out now. A vote of confidence from you lot is the kiss of death'. They had confidence in me all right: a week later I was given the push. They wished me a happy new year one day and gave me the sack the next. I think some of the people at board level at first resented Doug Ellis coming in from rivals Birmingham and taking over. Ellis was a good man in many ways and had a good side to him. But he wanted the image of a top man and was always willing to argue the toss. If you told Doug anything his first reaction was to be against it. All the boardroom squabbling and backbiting made it difficult to concentrate on achieving results. The fans were fed up and I was feeling the same way. When I joined them I felt I had something to build on. I did: shifting sand. However, I liked my stay at Villa. It's a big club and can and does compete with the best.

Bags packed, Docherty was soon heading for his first coaching job on the Continent with the Portuguese club Oporto on a one-year contract. Life was very different from the English game.

> I was told to coach the players and the club would handle the finances. If I wanted to sign a player I gave them his name and they did the rest. I had no involvement at all in transfers except to name the player I wanted. Portugal was a marvellous experience

for me. The weather was fantastic and we played a dozen or so games less than in England.

Having left Oporto at the end of his contract in 1971 Docherty returned to England with a golden goodbye from the Portuguese but no job. Things looked to be on an upswing when Manchester United sacked their manager Wilf McGuinness and Docherty was the hot tip to take over, but it was his old Preston team-mate Frank O'Farrell who got the job. Then Terry Neill, managing Hull City, got in touch and Docherty moved up as his assistant. At least it was a job. A week after arriving in Yorkshire, on a talent-spotting visit to Coventry, he met his old friend Tommy Cavanagh there on a similar mission; inside a few days Cavanagh had a phone call – Neill had a job for him at Hull as well.

Their first spell in management together was shortlived. Four months later Docherty confided to Cavanagh that he had been approached to manage Scotland on a trial basis but he was uncertain about taking on the challenge of managing the national team. 'I told him he was daft if he didn't take the job. It was a great opportunity for him and would put him back at the top. His career was at a very low ebb at that time, although Terry Neill was a smashing man to work for. The Scotland job was the turning point for Tommy. In fact, Hull was a lucky club for both of us because we both went on to bigger things from there.'

Docherty discussed the players Scotland had in the national squad . . . Billy Bremner, Eddie Gray, Frank McLintock, Peter Lorimer, Archie Gemmill . . . as the names rolled off Cavanagh noticed a glint in Docherty's eye. 'I could see the old enthusiasm returning at the prospect of working with such good players. He didn't need any more pushing.'

For his last club and its chairman, he was full of praise.

When I left Terry Neill at Hull to head for Scotland I was told by my Scottish bosses I was only on a three-match trial run. During that time Hull were marvellous to me and continued paying my wages. It was a magnificent gesture from the chairman, Harold Needler, and I couldn't thank him enough. I'll never say a wrong word about Hull City.

Docherty's reign as Scotland manager lasted less than fourteen months. In that short spell he revitalised his country's international standing after they had lost six of their previous seven games and drawn the other. And yet he guided them through just a dozen games, of which they won seven, drew two and lost only three. The three setbacks were just about palatable because they were against genuine world-class opposition – England, the scintillating Dutch side and the classy Brazilians in the 'mini World Cup' in South America. He started with a European Championship victory over Portugal and left also on a winning note, this time a World Cup win over Denmark, both at Hampden Park.

He was justifiably pleased with his record after setting out to put a smile back on the face of Scottish international football: 'I remember calling off our first practice match because no one could get the ball off wee Jimmy Johnstone.'

Docherty soon convinced the Scottish hierarchy he was the man for the job. His first game at Hampden Park in October 1971 produced a confidence-boosting victory 2–1 over Portugal with goals from John O'Hare and Archie Gemmill. The magic touch he felt had deserted him as his career slumped was back again. 'He was full of himself after that Scotland win over Portugal,' Cavanagh recalls. 'His old bounce and confidence came back.' The following month O'Hare was on the score sheet again, netting the only goal of the match to beat the Belgians at Aberdeen's Pittodrie stadium. The first defeat, in the third game, came against the fast-emerging Holland side in Amsterdam after Scotland had matched the superb Dutchmen throughout only to lose in the closing minute. The Scottish FA secretary Willie Allen had no doubt that the team had been unlucky. Immediately after the game he offered Docherty a four-year contract with a free hand to shape Scotland's international future.

Docherty put Scotland back on the road to success, but he pays ample tribute to the players he had to pick from. Apart from his dynamic skipper Billy Bremner there were other world-class men such as the two wingers, Peter Lorimer and Willie Morgan, the brilliant Kenny Dalglish, George Graham, Archie Gemmill and Asa Hartford. He is sure that if Eddie Gray had not been injury-prone he could have named a team that would have challenged the best in the world, while he always regretted that injury robbed him of his first-choice goalkeeper, Arsenal's Bob Wilson. With everyone fully fit they would indeed have been a force to be reckoned with, but even so, he felt he still had enough quality to put Scotland firmly on the world stage.

In the summer of 1972 Docherty and a party of eighteen players left Glasgow airport bound for South America and the Independence Cup tournament. When they landed at dawn in Rio the party were given a familiar welcome by a pipe band formed from expatriates living there, but they soon realised they were on business despite the laughs and the gags. Docherty the disciplinarian took over as he laid down the ground rules for the trip: 'We are not here for a holiday. We're here to represent our country at football and I won't tolerate anyone messing about.' The players were also warned that random dope testing would take place. Docherty was determined his players would reach peak fitness but he realised they would respond much more willingly if they were also given time to relax. He introduced a routine of swimming sessions in the morning, a light lunch and then serious training in the afternoon. There was also a shopping trip to Copacabana where the local St Andrews Society showed them the shops and tourist attractions.

The opening game of the tournament was against Yugoslavia, in Belo Horizonte. In the Scotland team for the match were two players who would one day join Docherty at Manchester United and another who was already there: Martin Buchan had already been taken to Old Trafford by manager Frank O'Farrell, the man Docherty would eventually succeed, and the other two were Alex Forsyth, winning his first Scotland cap, and Willie Morgan. Scotland earned a creditable 2–2 draw, although Morgan missed a penalty. At the press conference Docherty was asked by a Brazilian reporter if it was true his players had an eye for the local girls; he replied that he would only worry if they started looking at the local men.

The tournament was now being dubbed in the press the mini World Cup, and Scotland next played a goalless draw against Czechoslovakia in Porto Alegre. Their only defeat came in their third game, against Brazil in Rio, Jairzinho scoring the only goal. Scotland were thus out of the competition, and unfortunately the trip ended on a sour note when Docherty created an uproar after the Brazil game when he accused the Brazilians of 'crude tactics'; whether or not that was the reason, the Scottish party were told they could not stay on for the finals. But, despite Scotland's disappointing playing record, Docherty felt the tournament had shown that his team had the potential to do well in the World Cup in two years' time.

Outside events, however, decreed that he was soon to hit the road south once again and that his days as Scotland's manager were numbered, although his influence would still be felt.

9 Shaking Up Old Trafford

The impact Docherty had on Scotland's national team had not gone unnoticed in England. Manchester United were struggling and manager Frank O'Farrell was apparently under threat of the sack. The bubbling Docherty, whose teams matched his personality, was just what United needed to lift the gloom over Old Trafford.

Nine days before Christmas 1972 he was a man in the right place at the right time. The place was Crystal Palace, where Manchester United were thrashed embarrassingly 0–5; the time was minutes after the final whistle in that game when the United top brass decided that Frank O'Farrell had to go. Docherty was on a scouting mission to check on the young Palace defender, Tommy Taylor. Bert Head, the Palace manager at the time, thought young Taylor was an outstanding prospect and had telephoned Docherty at home in Largs to invite him down to look at the lad.

The match was so one-sided that no sensible judgement would have been possible on any Palace player. Instead, the Scotland boss found himself called to one side by a United director for a private chat.

He told me that changes were going to be made at Old Trafford and asked me if I would be interested in the manager's job. I was taken totally by surprise and said to him, 'You already have a manager.' 'Yes,' he said, 'but we won't have one next week.' He explained that the following Tuesday was the day of the board meeting, and Frank O'Farrell's position was at the top of the agenda. I felt sorry for Frank. He was a pal of mine. But the writing was on the wall. United were in trouble and the humiliation at Crystal Palace had really been the last straw. It was obvious they would not put up with the situation much longer.

I'd always felt that my destiny lay at Old Trafford. Now the chance to manage the biggest club in British football was there for the taking. I didn't need a second prompting. I told the United director I would walk from Scotland to Old Trafford for the job. But I waited for the formalities to be discussed in the correct way before I could accept.

O'Farrell was United's third manager in two years as the club slid inexorably from former glories. The decline had begun after winning the European Cup in 1968, and in the four intervening years had become a challenge to the very spirit of Old Trafford until the Crystal Palace result left them bottom but one of the first division; relegation, for the first time in thirty-seven years, was staring them in the face. It has been said that O'Farrell's failure was lack of communication. Seemingly chained to his desk, he stood apart from the staff and rarely mixed in even the most cursory way with any of them. A quiet, withdrawn man, summed up by one leading player after his departure in the words, 'He came as a stranger and went as a stranger.' The same could never be said of the man who was now in line to replace him.

Docherty was still in a daze when he headed back to his home in Scotland. He now had to hold his breath for three days until the crucial Manchester United board meeting. He waited by the phone, wondering as the time ticked by if there had been a last-minute snag and the offer had fallen through.

Then the telephone rang. It was the United director who'd spoken to me in the Crystal Palace boardroom the previous Saturday. He said, 'Tommy, we've just sacked Frank O'Farrell. Do you still want the job here?' For a second or two I didn't know what to say. Then it sank in that I was being offered the job I'd wanted since I first went into management at Chelsea. I said, 'I certainly do, but please speak to the Scottish people about it so we don't tread on any toes.'

Docherty had been given a free hand during his reign as Scotland manager and he wanted to leave on good terms with his bosses, wanted nothing done which would cause offence to the Scottish hierarchy. The United director agreed without hesitation, and promised everything would be sorted out in the right way.

The next morning the United chairman, Louis Edwards, acted swiftly. He telephoned Willie Allen and made a formal request to approach Docherty.

Willie Allen told me United had been on for permission to speak with me. He was tremendous about it and wished me well, and said there would be no objections to me talking to Louis Edwards. That was a magnificent gesture. My contract with Scotland still had two years to run, and he could have been difficult.

On the Thursday evening, just forty-eight hours after O'Farrell's sacking, Docherty flew into Manchester. He was met off the plane by Louis Edwards and Sir Matt Busby. It was the moment a dream came true. By the time they had walked to Edwards's Rolls-Royce they had shaken hands on a deal.

Candidly he admits he had two reasons for leaving the Scotland job: the money and the day-to-day involvement that is part of club management.

United paid me £15,000 a year, twice as much as Scotland, and I took the view that pride does not feed kids. But though the money was very important I could not resist the chance of joining a club as big as United and being involved in day-to-day deals and having money to spend on players. The national job couldn't offer that.

The next day he met the players. Then he walked onto the pitch and looked around the empty stadium and felt instantly at home. He would have his problems, however. This was a once-great team destroyed by three years of struggle and muddle; there were cobwebs to blow away and he meant to do just that. It was a process that would not be without trauma; but after his fashion he determined to get on with the job regardless and without delay. Back in his office he straightaway got down to planning for his first game, against Leeds United at Old Trafford. A lot was expected of him and there was plenty of interest being drummed up in the press. The previous weekend's thrashing at Crystal Palace still angered everyone, but he told the team to roll up their sleeves and get stuck in.

United drew 1–1 after a gutsy performance and the fans chanted, 'There's only one Tommy Docherty' as he left the dug-out at the final whistle. In the following weeks he was quickly aware of the problems surrounding the team.

Some of the players thought Old Trafford was a holiday camp. They were taking big money out of the club but giving nothing in return. I sensed there was a clique who thought they were running the club. I think some of the players had helped to get rid of Frank O'Farrell. We had many household names at Old Trafford, but some were coming towards the end of their careers at the top and obviously they didn't like being told so. Good players know it, but no famous player who is coming to the end of his career likes to be told he's no longer up to the standard required. We had some stars who were more interested in how *long* they played, not how *well* they played. We paid top money to the players, and the fans handed over their hard-earned cash at the turnstiles, and they deserved the best. I was determined to give it to them.

The youth policy was in a healthy state but the young lads were not being given their chance to blossom. A club renowned for its Busby Babes should not do that. Youth had always been given its fling at Old Trafford. Sir Matt had always made sure of that policy, and look at the dividends it had paid. The older players in the first team who were going over the hill were stopping the flow of youngsters coming through. The

team was stagnating. I had to change that or the club
would have become a laughing stock.

One of his first acts was to bring Tommy Cavanagh
over from Hull to be in charge of coaching and training.
Docherty told him that the team had to be rebuilt if it was
to get among the honours again. Cavanagh insists, 'Some
of the older players were not as good as they used to be
and there were others who were mediocre. Docherty has
never been given the full credit he deserves for rebuilding
United.'

One of the toughest decision facing Docherty was how
to deal with the big-name stars as he rebuilt the team.
'He was prepared to do that and it took courage. He
could make decisions and didn't worry about whether he
would be unpopular if he felt it would improve the team.
And he didn't like yes-men around him. He preferred to
hear what you really thought rather than have you say
something just to agree with him. I had many rows and
run-ins with him when I disagreed with what he was doing.
But when he arrived at United he felt the future of the
club lay in the young players and was determined to give
them their chance. He was tremendous in handling the
kids and encouraging them.'

Docherty fully grasped the difficulties he would encoun-
ter. The political pressures in and around the club were
intense and he knew Sir Matt Busby was the man some
players would run to if he made rash judgements in the
delicate job of breaking the mould of recent years. It
was essential to his authority that he got the backing of

the directors. He was to find they never interfered with his running of team matters, they always listened if he wanted to buy a player, and generally were 'a marvellous board and always gave me their backing'.

The man who dominated the club, of course, was the towering figure of Sir Matt Busby whose name over the years had become synonymous with Manchester United and its success. His pedigree was unquestionable and his influence permeated every corridor at Old Trafford. The Busby legend was already written throughout the football world and was deeply etched in the club's psyche. Busby the manager when United became the first English club to lift the European Cup of Champions in 1968; Busby the author of the famous youth policy at Old Trafford which led to his brilliant youngsters in the 1950s being indelibly tagged the Busby Babes; Busby the survivor – just – of the tragic air crash in which so many of his young stars perished on the slush-covered runway at Munich; Busby who had lain at death's door for weeks before his remarkable recovery. 'I looked up to Sir Matt,' admits Docherty. 'He was a giant in the game and respected by everyone inside and outside of Manchester United. He had built United's repuation world-wide. He was a man I wanted on my side.'

Only once in his four and a half years at Old Trafford did Docherty cross swords with Matt Busby. During a club holiday in Spain the chairman, Louis Edwards, threw a party in his room and Docherty went along for a drink with his players. The next day he was pulled to one side by Busby and warned of the dangers. 'He told me that familiarity breeds contempt. I reminded him that he played golf every Sunday morning with several of my players and when he did I felt the same way. He didn't like what I said, I could tell, but I know he took my point.'

Docherty soon found that the club was full of politics, fostered largely by a group of supporters who were on friendly terms with some of the directors and players and who thought they had real influence. 'We called them the "junior board". They were a poisonous lot.' He quickly understood, when he started the rebuilding of the team and had to sort out the big-name players, just how venomous they would be. 'It was then the whispering campaign started, with people egged on by the "junior board".'

Docherty was faced with hard decisions on the playing staff and he knew he would have to endure the tittle-tattle and backbiting, especially from the 'junior board'. He was to get encouragement from an unlikely source which would convince him that he was on the right lines with his plans to break up the team. Bobby Charlton was United's biggest star name and stood out world-wide as a shining example of sportsmanship and good sense.

Bobby came to me one day and told me he'd decided to retire from playing. He asked my permission to inform the chairman and directors. Bobby was still a very good player, but I would not have wanted to be the manager to ask him to hang up his boots. It was a marvellous gesture from a magnificent servant of the club. I wish some of his team-mates had behaved like he did. But then, Bobby was man enough to accept the situation as it was.

The ever modest Charlton, his fair hair thinning now, still moved with all the majesty and authority of a ship in full sail when he played his final League game in April 1973, against Chelsea at Stamford Bridge. In a career stretching back twenty years he had become recognised all over the world as a chivalrous and scrupulously fair opponent, and was booked only once. Just about every honour and medal in the game had come his way, but nothing had diminished his commitment to Manchester United.

Docherty's problems were immense as *The Times* recognised after United had lost 1–3 to Arsenal at Highbury:

Arsenal 3 Manchester United 1
from The Times of January 8 1973

A sympathetic audience is the easiest to satisfy, so Manchester United had only to stay on their feet to be cheered like champions at Arsenal on Saturday. They collapsed 3–1; expensive noses buried in Highbury's mud; sympathy lost because even devotees of the United cult recognised shoddy workmanship.

Tommy Docherty's most urgent job is not necessarily to sign more cheques but to rid the club of selfish apathy that manifests itself in players refusing to take responsibility for mistakes while imploring everyone to acknowledge moments of individual success. Several of them wanted to take the curtain call before acting in the play.

Docherty is aware of the problem, especially after having it shouted at him by the example of Arsenal's selfless teamwork. The comparison was too clearly defined to be ignored. Arsenal began as if expecting United to be unrecognisably rejuvenated by two new players and a new manager. When they discovered that their former colleague, Graham, was responsible for most of United's 'grafting' they must have appreciated the irony. Here was a player, criticised at Highbury for not taking his share of the work, burying his better attack-making talents for the sake of his team.

United were unlucky in that two of Arsenal's goals might have been saved if Stepney had not been confused by mistakes in defence, but they were also in no way deserving of better fortune. When they deluded themselves into thinking that Arsenal could be held to a goalless draw, they produced a defensive fiasco. It was like trying to bail out a boat without first fixing the hole.

Kennedy's first-half goal might have been stopped by Stepney if Young had not accidentally diverted the shot. Soon after half-time, Stepney was again deceived by his own defenders as they tried to stop Kennedy playing the ball down for Armstrong to shoot in. Arsenal then played so efficiently, and sometimes so attractively, that they rowed over United's pressure. Moore should have scored when he made six yards of clear space in the Arsenal penalty area. But there was not one United player to compare with Simpson and Storey, who were positive, committed and determined.

Arsenal had to score again. Armstrong, having a superb game, centred and Ball dived for a fine headed goal. Not surprisingly Arsenal relaxed when clearly unbeatable and Kidd scored for United in the last few minutes. A disproportionate number of United players wanted to take the credit.

Arsenal: Wilson; Rice, NcNab; Storey, Blockley, Simpson; Armstrong, Ball, Radford, Kennedy, Kelly

Manchester United: Stepney; Young, Forsyth; Graham, Sadler, Buchan; Morgan, Kidd, Charlton, Law, Moore

Nothing, however, not even (or perhaps *especially*) the 'junior board' could stop the Docherty whirlwind once it was under way. In his first month he splashed out over £500,000 on five players – four Scotsmen and one Irishman. George Graham was signed from Arsenal for £125,000; Partick Thistle got £100,000 for the 20-year-old defender Alex Forsyth; centre-half Jim Holton came from Shrewsbury for £80,000, while another £30,000 was spent on Mick Martin from Bohemians. The most expensive signing was Lou Macari, who cost £200,000 from Celtic.

Two days after signing, Macari scored on his debut in United's 2–2 draw with West Ham at Old Trafford which lifted the club off the bottom of the table. But a 4–1 defeat at Ipswich in February brought back relegation fears. In

March Docherty bought Gerry Daly from Bohemians as he searched for young talent with which to rebuild. But United continued to struggle among a cluster of clubs at the bottom of the table, separated by just 1 point. Then victory over Newcastle was followed by a draw at Spurs and a crucial win at Southampton and the team eased itself up the table and into safety.

Charlton's departure was a deeply moving occasion, memorably recorded in this report:

Chelsea 1 Manchester United 0
from The Times April 30 1973

When Chelsea beat Manchester United by a single goal on Saturday the season not only ended at Stamford Bridge but the League career of football's first gentleman – Bobby Charlton – was brought to a close.

What neat touches there were came from Osgood; the rest as always belonged to Hollins and to two young Chelsea wingers, Brolly and Britton, fledglings who may yet prove to be an integral part of the new Stamford Bridge. The goal itself and the end of a lazy, sleepy hour somehow symbolised the match. As Baldwin flicked on a long diagonal pass from Hollins, Osgood breasted down the ball, left Holton stranded, and pushed it slowly like some reluctant snail past Stepney's confused dive by way of knee and toe.

For the rest it was merely an afternoon of nostalgia, for this was Charlton's farewell, his 604th League game, a first-division record. The gates were closed half an hour before the start and every available inch of a fractured ground in the process of reconstruction was taken by a 44,000 crowd. Both teams provided a guard of honour for the man himself as he took the stage alone.

There was the presentation of an inscribed silver cigarette box by the Chelsea chairman: photographers gathered like seagulls on some harbour wall behind Bonetti's posts in the hope of recording a final goal by the master at the end of a career nearly twenty years long, begun symbolically against Charlton Athletic and ended now at Stamford Bridge – a sentimental bridge across the years.

A handshake all round the players at the end, a wave to the packed terraces and he was gone, thankfully perhaps, since he was not one for nostalgic junketings. As the crowd chanted 'Sir Bobby Charlton', one watched the passing of a man the brash modern age hungered for and found – the great performer of his time who was also a hero and a human being, gentle, chivalrous, wise.

Chelsea: Bonetti; Ron Harris, McCreadie; Hollins, Hinton, Droy; Britton, Baldwin, Osgood, Kember, Brolly

Manchester United: Stepney; Young, Sidebottom; Graham, Holton, Buchan; Morgan, Kidd, Charlton, Macari, Martin

At the end of 1973–74, Docherty's first full season in charge, United had slipped into the second division.

Doubtless the FA Cup was the subject of discussion between Tommy Docherty and Bill Nicholson after Spurs had beaten Chelsea 2–1 in the 66–67 final.

17 Bobby Tambling, Chelsea's No. 11, puts the ball past Sprake in a match against Leeds United at Stamford Bridge in 1966–67. The other Chelsea player to the right of Tambling is George Graham and Paul Madeley, Willie Bell and Jack Charlton are in the picture for Leeds.

18 Peter Bonetti dives in vain to stop one of the two Spurs goals entering the Chelsea net during the 1966–67 FA Cup final at Wembley. The Spurs goals were scored by Robertson and Saul.

Tommy Docherty, the newly-appointed manager of Manchester United at
ristmas 1972.

20 Docherty galvanised the Scotland side when he was appointed manager in 1971, being given complete control over team and selection matters. Only three of Scotland's first ten matches under Docherty's command were lost.

21 Steve Coppell takes the ball away from Colin Todd in the Manchester United v Derby County FA Cup semi-final at Hillsborough, won 2–0 by United, in 1976. United went on to lose unexpectedly to Southampton in the final.

Peter Osgood, transferred from Chelsea to Southampton, takes on
ewart Houston and Brian Greenhoff in the 1976 FA Cup final, which
uthampton won 1–0.

Martin Buchan, bought by Frank O'Farrell from Aberdeen in 1972 for
30,000, played consistently well for Docherty at centre-back for United.
ere he clears the ball under pressure during a United v Manchester City
atch during the 1976–77 season.

24 Laurie Brown and Tommy Docherty leap in triumph as the whistle blows on United's victory by 2–0 over Leeds United at Hillsborough in the FA Cup semi-final of 1977.

25 Lou Macari, hands aloft, sees his shot deflected by Jimmy Greenhoff past right-back Neal with the goalkeeper, Ray Clemence, out of position, to win the FA Cup for United 2–1 against Liverpool in 1977.

United, led by Alex Stepney, celebrate their Wembley FA Cup final
ctory against Liverpool by 2–1 in 1977. From left to right, Jimmy
reenhoff, Brian Greenhoff (partly obscured), Sammy McIlroy, Jimmy
choll, Alex Stepney, Gordon Hill, Tommy Docherty, Tommy Cavanagh.

Tommy Docherty and Tommy Cavanagh, friends and colleagues since
eir early days at Preston, together again at Old Trafford soon after
ocherty's arrival at Manchester United.

28 Sir Matt Busby and Tommy Docherty soon after the latter's arrival at Old Trafford in 1972.

The season started ominously with defeat at Arsenal while across the city at Maine Road, Manchester City were beating Birmingham 3–1, helped by two goals from Scottish international Denis Law who had left United after a rift with Docherty. The team continued to struggle, and in December skipper George Graham was dropped along with Lou Macari as Docherty tried to find a successful blend. The team's poor form continued with seven defeats in ten games while City had reached the League Cup final and named Law in their team.

In a bid to beat the drop Jim McCalliog (who had sought a transfer from Chelsea under Docherty) was bought from Wolves for £60,000 but was injured in the opening minutes of his debut at Birmingham in the middle of March as United lost 0–1 to sink deeper into relegation trouble. At the end of the month a morale-boosting win at Chelsea was followed by a draw with Burnley and another crucial win at Norwich as United fought for survival. McCalliog scored twice in a 3–1 win against Everton in mid-April, but defeat at Goodison Park later in the month left United again on the edge of the precipice. The issue was still uncertain as United faced neighbours City in the final home game of the season. Even victory would still mean relegation if results were unfavourable for United in the matches involving fellow strugglers Birmingham and West Ham.

Nearly 60,000 packed Old Trafford and watched as, seven minutes from time, Colin Bell linked with Francis Lee who threaded a pass towards the United penalty area where Law backed-heeled the only goal of the game. The stadium erupted and referee David Smith abandoned the game with three minutes left as fans invaded the pitch.

**Manchester United 0 Manchester City 1
from The Times of April 29 1974**

The saddest moment of Saturday's debâcle at Old Trafford, where the match was abandoned with Manchester City leading United 1–0, came when Sir Matt Busby appealed to the crowd to get off the pitch so that the game could finish. 'For the sake of the club', he said.

Here was a man who had made Manchester United one of the greatest club sides in the world, and who had led them to a series of unprecedented triumphs. Now, his team already doomed to second-division football, he was faced with the additional ignominy of appealing to thousands of hooligans to avoid the disgrace of having the match abandoned and the ground closed for a long period next season. Sir Matt's appeal had no effect. The match *was* abandoned, with three minutes left, and United *do* face the prospect of a long closure of their ground next season.

Most of us left Old Trafford, as the last few hundred hooligans were still stamping up and down on the pitch and Manchester United officials were talking about ten-foot-high fences round the ground, with a feeling of despair, not only for the future of Manchester United, but for the future of football itself.

For let us face it. The abandonment at Old Trafford was just another example of the way the mobs can influence the outcome of matches these days. Nobody can tell to what extent the players were intimidated by the crowd, before or during the match, but several were attacked and Corrigan, the City goalkeeper, claimed later to have been struck by a flying dart.

Shortly before the kick-off there were hundreds of ruffians ranting and raving in the middle of the pitch. The police managed to clear them off so that a start could be made, but there was always the probability that a single incident would bring them on again.

So it proved. Late in the second half Manchester City scored the goal they had been threatening to score all afternoon, Law cleverly back-heeling the ball in from Lee's pass. Immediately the crowd were on the pitch, not from the Stretford End, where the United supporters were tightly packed, but from the more thinly populated opposite end. Seconds later they were joined by the crowds flooding on from the Stretford end. The game was halted, restarted for a few minutes, during which time Law was substituted, then finally abandoned with the crowds once more surging on to the field, fights breaking out all over the terraces, and one goal partly obscured by smoke from a fire.

If the mob went on to the pitch with the idea of preventing defeat and relegation they were disappointed, for the results of other first-division matches made the score at Old Trafford immaterial. In any case, the score is almost bound to be allowed to stand.

If there is one consolation to be squeezed from Saturday's sad affair it is that the behaviour of the players and the referee, Dave Smith, was beyond reproach. Assuming the score is allowed stand, City were well worth the victory, for they carried a much greater threat in attack, and defended better. Doyle was outstanding at the back; Lee, Law, and Summerbee all had their moments up front.

It was Tueart, however, who proved to be the most effective striker, hitting the bar once and forcing a fine save from Stepney shortly afterwards.

United started off well enough but their old failing in front of goal soon became apparent. Morgan, left with far too much to do, switched his tactics in a vain effort to prize open the City defence.

Manchester United: Stepney; Forsyth, Houston; Brian Greenhoff, Holton, Buchan; Morgan, Macari, McIlroy, McCalliog, Daly

Manchester City: Corrigan; Barrett, Donachie; Doyle, Booth, Oakes; Summerbee, Bell, Lee, Law, Tueart

United were down. It was a disaster for such a big club, and Sir Matt and Louis Edwards made it very clear that they did not like it. Docherty expected the sack, but despite their anger the directors were unaminous in their support of him, gave him a dozen bottles of champagne and told him to get on with getting the club back into the premier division. 'It was a marvellous gesture and I was able to face my critics with confidence.'

The directors were to reap handsome dividends from their determination to stand by their manager. The following season United mesmerised the second division while bouncing straight back to the first on a wave of high-octane performances which inflated crowds wherever they played as they swept through to the second-division Championship.

> My philosophy was to let the boys express themselves, just as I had done with my young Chelsea players years before. We sparkled with wonderful, entertaining football in our season in the second division, and the fans loved it and poured through the turnstiles to watch us.

His players were able to express themselves because they were freed from defensive constraints. Attack was the watchword which Docherty brought to Old Trafford, he would have none of the ways of other managers who would close the game up as soon as they went into the lead. 'This defensive football is a bore. Spectators want to watch goals. That is what we try to supply.'

Even when losing badly his teams did not fall back on to a packed defensive wall. Beaten 0–3 at Ipswich, Docherty was still able to say:

> I am proud of my lads. They kept trying to score away from home and they never went on the defensive. Someone has to lose, so why not give the fans something to remember? We didn't like losing – who does? But we lost and could still keep our heads up because we didn't pull all our men back. The only aim in football is to score goals, and if in defeat we

score fewer than our opponents that's just the way it happens.

It was to soccer's detriment that others did not follow the example but stuck to safety-first.

In the summer Docherty paid £200,000 to his former club Hull City for striker Stuart Pearson. It was a move which would pay rich dividends. Pearson hit the target immediately, scoring on his début in the 4–0 win over Orient. He scored again in the first home game of the season, a thumping 4–0 victory over Millwall when Gerry Daly scored a hat-trick. United roared on with five wins and two draws in their opening seven games to lead the table by 4 points.

The Docherty express raced on as the team dominated the second-division promotion race. Macari scored the goal in a 1–0 victory at Southampton in April which ensured promotion; then two weeks later United clinched the second-division Championship, ending a run of ten games unbeaten with a 2–2 draw at Notts County. The champagne corks were popping at Old Trafford at the end of April as they crushed Blackpool 4–0 in the final game of the season. Pearson scored twice and Macari got a goal as they ended the campaign joint leading scorers with eighteen goals each. The season had produced a massive sixty-six goals, and a million fans and more had poured into Old Trafford. Docherty, the villain of relegation, was the hero again.

The following year, 1975–76, United challenged strongly for a League and Cup double. Liverpool, though, proved just too strong as they took the Championship with United four points behind in third place.

However, Docherty's team had reached the FA Cup final. Two spectacular goals from winger Gordon Hill in the semi-final had beaten the more experienced and hotly tipped Derby County 2–0 to set up the Wembley showdown with second-division underdogs Southampton. Two former Chelsea players who had played under Docherty were in the Southampton team, Peter Osgood and Jim McCalliog (this time the Scotsman had lasted only eleven months under the Docherty banner), but it was the relatively unknown Bobby Stokes who stole the show. McCalliog's pass sent him through the United defence six minutes from time to score the only goal of the game and create one of the biggest Cup upsets in years.

Within a year United and Docherty were back and upsetting the odds themselves. En route to the 1977 Cup final United had met the holders Southampton again and took revenge for their final defeat of the previous season, though it was a tough hurdle. The first match of the fifth round produced a 2–2 draw at the Dell before United went through 2–1 in the Old Trafford replay. Another 2–1 victory over Leeds in the semi-finals at Hillsborough set up a Wembley date with Liverpool, who were chasing a magnificent treble of League Championship, FA Cup and European Cup.

Before then, however, another major adjustment to the team had to be made. Gerry Daly, an instinctive and creative midfield player, went to Derby County and thus created a problem. The answer lay in the buying of Brian

Greenhoff's brother Jimmy from Stoke and thus acquiring a clever and experienced striker to take the weight off Pearson in the centre of the attack. At the same time McIlroy was switched to midfield in place of Daly. The moves worked like a charm, and for most of the 1976–77 season United were up with Liverpool, Manchester City, Ipswich, Newcastle and Aston Villa in the race for the League Championship. They eventually finished sixth, a slight fall from the previous year, but they gained a place in Europe for the second year running. For the second successive year too they got to Wembley.

This time it was United's turn to spring the surprise as they won 2–1. However, the match only really came alive after the interval. In the first half United fell back into uncharacteristic defence and surrendered the midfield; only the composure of Brian Greenhoff, Buchan and Albiston saved them from virtual annihilation. Five minutes into the second half it all suddenly took on the drama and colour expected at Wembley when Jimmy Greenhoff back-headed to Pearson who, shooting from an unlikely angle, still beat Ray Clemence. The expected Liverpool counterpunch came within three minutes through Case. It took only another two minutes before Macari shot for goal, the ball rebounded off Jimmy Greenhoff wide of Clemence, and Docherty was at last assured of a Wembley win. United had triumphed in a style which had the critics acclaiming them for their 'adventure and flair in attack'. Liverpool, denied the treble chance, went on to win the European Cup to add to their League title.

After the bitter disappointment of defeat the previous

year by Southampton Docherty was jubilant. 'We beat the best team in Europe when we beat Liverpool. I felt we could go on from there and take more honours.'

How had the players fared in face of the Docherty tornado? An early casualty, and perhaps the most notable, was Denis Law, who was given a free transfer to Manchester City. McCalliog came and went within a year. Trevor Anderson, inherited from O'Farrell, was dispensed with after a brief while. Willie Morgan fell out with Docherty and returned to Burnley. The brilliant Gerry Daly, having been brought in by Docherty, eventually clashed with him and left. And most oddly, George Graham came, helped to avoid relegation, but was dropped in a swap for Portsmouth's ageing Ron Davies – who was never to start a game for United; it was one of Docherty's more bizarre deals.

10 Past his Best

As ever around this time, George Best was making his presence felt at Old Trafford, both in his appearances and his increasing disappearances, and Docherty's relationship with him is interesting – two larger-than-life, out-of-the-rut characters coming face to face.

The Best legend was well established: the footballing genius, and the hedonist pursuing beautiful women, fast cars, business deals and sun-soaked Spanish playgrounds. Frank O'Farrell, in despair, was reported as saying that, when fit, Best was one of the finest players in the world, and thus he pinpointed the problem: not even Best could display his full range of talents unless he trained hard and kept at peak fitness.

O'Farrell must have realised that any attempt to discipline the young Ulsterman or to leave him out of the struggling team would need some explaining to the United faithful. On the other hand there were voices urging him to grasp the nettle and give him the push. There were newspaper stories that Best had been warned to stay out of the night clubs and be home in his digs before midnight, but by December 1972 boiling point had been reached. Early in the month Best missed training and was actually dropped for a game at Norwich; the team slipped into the bottom three of the first division; the board lost patience; O'Farrell was given a record pay-off and Best, sacked with him, drove off in a white Rolls-Royce vowing never to play for United again.

Tommy Docherty was now the one in charge. When the wandering hero became ill and returned from Spain early in 1973, he persuaded him to give it one more try. He recalls the events leading up to the return of Best.

Sir Matt and Paddy Crerand [briefly Docherty's assistant] wanted George back at Old Trafford and a meeting was arranged with him at a house in nearby Sale belonging to a friend of the club. All credit to Sir Matt; he left me to handle the discussion with Best, but really I was already keen on his return. We didn't have too many good players at United at that time. George was a proven genius as a player and I felt he could still do a good job for us. A great player like Best never loses his skill or his class and George hadn't been out of the game too long. We wanted him back and the lad himself wanted to come back. It was as simple as that. He was easy to talk to and here was a glorious opportunity to bring a great player and a great club together again.

Docherty recognised that Best had been having problems. He'd returned from Spain fearing for his life after a thrombosis in a leg. He would need nursing back.

I told him I fully understood his position and that I wouldn't expect too much of him straightaway. The buzz around Old Trafford [when the news came out] was incredible. I really thought I could motivate him again. Best was just the tonic I wanted to lift the club and its fans. He was a smashing lad but he most certainly had been handled in the wrong way over the years. He mixed with the wrong people and did as he pleased. He was such a great player he could get away with almost anything, and that was the mistake. The club should have kept him on a tighter rein for his own good and the good of United. As it was, he was allowed too much scope and began letting people down too often.

With other superstars like Bobby Charlton, Denis Law, Paddy Crerand and Nobby Stiles also at the club, Docherty believed the situation had been allowed to drift out of control.

Sir Matt Busby loved the game and he always wanted his players to enjoy themselves. He possibly believed that he could get the best out them by giving them freedom to express themselves. I think with hindsight he went too far in that direction. There was no real discipline in the team. With a firmer hand I think the club would have won even more honours. Players with outstanding skills, like George Best, thought their natural talent would pull them through. But if you don't work hard in training then it doesn't.

Docherty is saddened that the situation was allowed to go on without any lessons being learned when Wilf McGuinness took over from Busby as manager and inherited what amounted to 'player power'. McGuinness often said how little control he had in dealing with the players. Apparently Wilf had to put up with all sorts of misdemeanours and breaches of club discipline from George Best, and often felt like sending him home, on one occasion even before an important Cup-tie. But Sir Matt always thought the team could not do without Best.

It was against this background that Docherty was willing to lay out the welcome mat once again for Best to return to Old Trafford in 1973. Without doubt Best was the player to pull the fans back through the turnstiles. The club couldn't lose no matter what the outcome, and if it worked out the potential benefits for both team and club were enormous. There were – of course – stories about the vast amount of money he was being paid. In fact, he was on just £150 a week and that was less than the team captain, Willie Morgan. Docherty made a pact with him.

I told him I would keep his problems away from people. 'Do it for me on the park and I'll protect you off it.' I promised him that, and he agreed. I also told him that if he missed training in the mornings I would overlook it if he made up for it in the afternoon by training alone. That was very important for him to retain his match fitness.

I didn't have any rows with George or problems with him. After three or four games I could see all the old skill was still there. He could still beat people. But he couldn't go away from them, he had lost that vital extra yard of pace that had separated him from ordinary players. I could see the fear in his face. I think he knew he was not as good as he had been. No player could lead the life he had been leading and still perform with his level of skill on the park. I think it frightened him. I remember a game at Queen's Park Rangers. We were hammered 4–0. I pulled George off at half-time because he just wasn't doing it for us. He didn't like it but he knew deep down he couldn't do it any more.

He was a quiet lad. He never flared up. A very nice lad to work with. But he was a spent genius.

How far was I expected to go to keep him if he was no longer doing it on the park or off it? You can't train and booze. The reason he trained sometimes in the afternoons was because he couldn't get up in the morning. I couldn't even contact him. I didn't know where he was living. He just left telephone numbers with friends. People used to ring the club and ask where George was because he'd promised to do this and that but had let them down – he couldn't say 'no'; if someone asked him to do something he would agree to get them off his back. But we simply couldn't enlighten them, because we didn't know where he was or what he was doing most of the time. As far as I knew he could have been in Manchester, London or Spain. Remember, Spain was his favourite haunt and he flew off there whenever he felt like it.

We had no option really but to treat George as an adult. But he had too many personal problems. He's a smashing lad, when he's not drinking. George Best is to blame for himself. A lot of people wanted to help and tried to help him. I think you could live with Best for a hundred years and still not know him.

Docherty's silence over the real reason for Best finally leaving United was broken when Best lambasted him in a book. United were playing Plymouth Argyle in the opening round of the FA Cup. Docherty always insisted the players must report to the grill room at Old Trafford for a pre-match meal at 11.30 on Saturday mornings, three and a half hours before kick-off.

I had picked George in the team and wasn't too worried when he didn't arrive for lunch. When he still hadn't arrived at 2.30 I was forced to alter the team because I had to hand in the team sheet. I really had no option but to leave him out. Twenty minutes before kick-off there was a knock on the dressing-room door and there was George, arm in arm with a girl.

I said to him, 'I'm sorry you're too late. I've altered the team.' I told him I would talk to him after the game. He mumbled, but he wasn't stroppy in any way. But he didn't look in a fit state to play football. He didn't argue, just turned away with his girl on his arm, and I never saw him again.

After that clubs used to ring me at Old Trafford asking if they could take George 'on loan'. It became a farce, with George the star of a fair-ground show. We got so fed up with it we released him altogether. That way George got the money for any appearances he made and no one lost. After all, he had cost United nothing. He had also given the club marvellous service in his heyday, no one can deny him that. So Sir Matt and the board decided to let him go for his own good.

Docherty dismisses the claim by Best that the two of them met in the referee's changing-room before the fateful Plymouth Argyle tie: 'Why would I want to do that? It would have been a foolish place to hold such a private meeting. The room was exclusively for the use of the referee. No way would I have taken George in there when there were plenty of places in the club where we could have had a private chat'. Best got something else wrong, insists Docherty: 'George apparently claimed I did not meet him early enough to tell him he was being dropped. That is nonsense because I fully intended playing him and had named him on my team sheet. I scratched his name out when he had not turned up with half an hour to go before the kick-off when I had to give the referee the team sheet.'

Best, of course, had many admirers, and some claimed that Docherty felt threatened, although the idea seemed backed more by mischief-making than fact.

I did not mind one bit a player being bigger than me if that was what they thought. When all's said and done, as a manager you are only as big as your players. If they succeed for you on the park you all benefit. It was the fault of George and no one else that he missed the Plymouth Cup-tie. And it was a sad day for the club and me personally when we finally parted company with him. We knew he would drink when he came back to us and would struggle to get up in the morning. But we all wanted him to succeed . . . that would have been one of the greatest draws in football.

11 Resign, or Else . . .

United's surprising defeat of Liverpool to win the 1977 FA Cup was the climax of Docherty's tempestuous career at United. The euphoria of that occasion wove a spell around Docherty, the club and its supporters for they knew that greatness had come again. The match itself was reported as follows:

FA Cup Final 1977
Manchester United 2 Liverpool 1
from The Times of May 23 1977

After a distinguished season in which they had come to expect victory even on their poorer days, Liverpool suffered the rare irony of playing well and losing in Saturday's excellent FA Cup final at Wembley. With their 2–1 defeat by Manchester United went the hopes of an illustrious treble, also embracing the Championship and European Cup. Too much was expected of them and when the moment came to draw on the strength that had previously been so reliably summoned, there was not enough left.

Yet this was not a day when sympathy ranked high

among the emotions. Liverpool had already enjoyed one prize-giving when retaining the Championship title and on Wednesday in Rome they may revive their spirits in time to lift the European Cup in another final against Borussia Mönchen Gladbach. Such is their proven resilience that the tears of disappointment can quickly turn to those of pleasure. The treble would have been the fully ripened fruit of a decade but perhaps it was too perfect, too tidy for the very unpredictable game of football.

Similarly, it would have been a less interesting Cup final had the majority of predictions been satisfied. On the day little went according to preconceptions except the fulfilment of hopes for a match to restore the full value of the occasion. Although Liverpool set off in character, carefully preparing their ground, they expanded into an attacking style far earlier than was expected. Manchester United began by looking better than at any time in their defeat by Southampton a year before but, surprisingly, it was doing what came unnaturally, defending, that formed a foundation for victory.

Near the end of a first half of sufficient if quiet interest the feeling was that United were ill-equipped for the second when Liverpool could hardly fail to take the chances they were making. United had conceded midfield and were magnificently saved from a slaughter by the composure of Brian Greenhoff, Buchan and Albiston, the young replacement for Houston.

The proposal that Liverpool would do no more than absorb United's attacks until well into the second half was clearly not their own. Kennedy's header down towards the near corner of United's goal was instantly thrust away by Stepney's foot or else they would have received rightful reward for unquestionable superiority, but as the half ended Jimmy Greenhoff was almost able to score as a direct result of a careless interception by Hughes. It was the loudest whisper of encouragement for United since Hill made Clemence turn his menacing centre on to the crossbar after a quarter of an hour.

Five minutes into the second half the match seemed to breast the hill and suddenly there was a new horizon, totally different to the one we had expected. Hughes and Smith failed to hold Jimmy Greenhoff, who had always troubled them. His back header dropped under Pearson's control but he was moving too wide. Clemence would surely cover the angle. The shot was too late, too close to Clemence and aimed at the remnants of a target at the near post. But the ball was well struck. Clemence was still moving too quickly to turn on his side and it hit the net before he fell.

As the 'Stretford End' at Wembley celebrated, one wondered whether this goal was not also the invitation to United's downfall. Liverpool's counter-punch is their speciality and, sure enough, within three minutes Case was allowed time to control a centre, turn and shoot past Stepney for another goal plucked from the eye of a crisis. It was at this moment that Liverpool would normally have begun to stride out. Here, though, their powers failed. In another two minutes Smith was caught out by the speed of Macari and Jimmy Greenhoff and his own advancing years. Macari came alongside in support of Greenhoff and took over. His shot hit Jimmy Greenhoff sufficiently hard to deflect wide of Clemence and into the goal.

Tension, too often the enemy of such occasions, now held the game in a fascinating grip. There was still plenty of time for Liverpool and too much for United. Buchan had the responsibility for planning Manchester's long defence. Liverpool planned their long attack from the bench. They withdrew Johnson and sent Callaghan into the field, but it was Fairclough, the unpredictable youngster being saved for Rome, who was really needed to challenge Brian Greenhoff's command in the penalty area. They missed more chances and so United survived. If Liverpool's dream was finished in five minutes, the day and domestic season was completed to perfection by the generosity of their players and supporters in defeat and the delight of United's manager, Tommy Docherty, at last a winner after eight visits to Wembley.

Liverpool: Clemence; Neal, Jones; Smith, Kennedy, Hughes; Keegan, Case, Heighway, Johnson, McDermott

Manchester United: Stepney; Nicholl, Albiston; McIlroy, Brian Greenhoff, Buchan; Coppell, Jimmy Greenhoff, Pearson, Macari, Hill

That same evening at the Royal Lancaster Hotel in London, as the celebration dinner was in full swing, Docherty was unable to relax. With the Wembley roar of success still alive in his head he was wrestling with a personal crisis.

Within months of his arrival at Old Trafford a close friendship began to develop with Mary Brown, wife of the club's physio, Laurie Brown. They used to meet at club functions and found a mutual attraction despite Docherty being seventeen years the older, but it was a long time before she agreed to go out with him. Slowly their friendship grew into a love affair.

It all began so innocently. It was just one of those things that happened over a long period of time as our feelings became stronger. I noticed how bored she seemed when she was with Laurie. In any case he didn't appear to be showing a lot of interest in her.

His own marriage was breaking up after twenty-seven years.

It wasn't the fault of my wife, Agnes. We had drifted apart, and I was being difficult. I know I couldn't have been easy to live with. I would have left home anyway, even if I hadn't been going with Mary.

The outwardly controlled Docherty felt far from calm. It came as almost a relief when Mary told him Laurie knew they were seeing one another ('Doc always takes the girls out,' he had laughed), but still there were pressures dictating that they kept it secret. They both had families to consider, for one thing, but there were wider implications.

Mary was very concerned that it might affect my job. I thought it was always a possibility that I might be

157

asked to resign if everything was brought into the
open, but I was willing to risk that to stay with Mary.

When the burden of secrecy became too much he turned
to his friend of over thirty years, Tommy Cavanagh.
The chance came when they were in London for an
international, and the revelation staggered Cavanagh,
but like a true friend he did not attempt to preach or
moralise. Instead he simply warned Docherty, 'Are you
sure you're doing the right thing – do you realise what a
big step you're taking?' It had been a relief to talk about
it, but now, on this Cup final night of triumph, he knew
the time had come when he could keep his United bosses
in the dark no longer. Both he and Mary had agreed it
was the only way forward. They also understood only too
well that the consequences for his career at Old Trafford
could be disastrous.

The next day Docherty returned to Manchester with
his players to a civic reception. 'I tried to act as normally
as I could. We were being treated like heroes by the fans,
but my mind was on other things.' He was pondering the
consequences of revelation: 'Once I'd plucked up the
courage to tell the United directors about me and Mary,
and I *mean* plucked up the courage, I knew I could be
laying my whole career on the line. There were plenty
of people in and around the club who wanted me out
anyway, and I knew the knives would be sharpened.'

Docherty moved decisively next morning to sort out
his private life. He telephoned Louis Edwards at home
in Alderley Edge, an exclusive suburb on the south side

of Manchester. The chairman's son, Martin, answered the call, and when he said his father was still celebrating the Cup win Docherty's first thought was to hang up and simply try to ride out the storm when his affair with Mary came to light.

The decision was taken from him when Martin Edwards went on, 'What is it, Tom, anything I can do?'

Docherty responded immediately. 'Martin, my marriage is on the rocks and I'm very involved with Mary Brown.'

There was a pause, then Docherty was able to relax a little as Martin responded, 'Tommy, that's a private matter. It's nothing to do with the club. What you do with your private life is your own business.'

For the first time since the Cup win Docherty felt genuinely at ease.

I believed at that point that things would turn out all right. I believed what Martin was telling me, but I think later on when the directors met at the chairman's house to decide my future they would all have had their own say and the situation changed. What was said and how they voted on my future I don't know to this day. But what I am sure of is that Big Louis was my pal and would have been on my side. He and I never had a cross word. I think he liked my brash style and my way of doing things. I could pull his leg and make him laugh. Occasionally we would go out socially and have a meal, a few drinks and a laugh together.

Docherty's telephone conversation with Martin Edwards may have brought him comfort but events were happening unknown to him which would turn up the heat. Word had got around, and a friend tipped him off that a national Sunday newspaper was about to break the story. It was now a matter of waiting for the inevitable. On the Sunday morning of 19 June his fears were amply confirmed with banner headlines detailing the 'Love Tangle Sensation'. There was also strong speculation that he would be sacked. 'Curiously enough, that part hurt me more than the story. My first thought was, "Why should I be sacked for falling in love?"'

Whatever his thoughts, he knew now that his fight for survival as manager of Manchester United was about to begin.

Defiantly he insisted he would be carrying on as manager of United. 'I'm staying, and you can quote me,' he told reporters when they came swarming. Louis Edwards was also proclaiming that Docherty would be staying and that the Mary Brown affair was a 'private matter.' Mary herself said to reporters with disarming honesty, 'I know it sounds corny . . . but I love him.' Pressed further, Docherty tried to head off more speculation by telling the hungry newsmen, 'I can still work with Laurie Brown.'

Of Mary he says, 'She was marvellous. If anything I was the one nearer to cracking up. But I know behind the brave face it must have been a very testing time for her.'

At least they were together and able to lend mutual support, because four days before the Sunday newspapers broke the story Docherty had gone to live with Mary at her mother's large 18th-century stone house in Broadbottom near Glossop, just twenty miles or so from Manchester. Mary had been living there with Laurie and their two children. When Docherty moved in it was agreed that he would live downstairs with Mary, while Laurie would live upstairs with the children. Mary's mother had her own self-contained quarters in another part of the house. Though certainly unconventional the arrangement at least was practical: it meant Mary could stay with her children, go upstairs each night, kiss them good night and tuck them into bed.

Docherty's future had been the big debate throughout and beyond football, fuelled by constant media speculation. He had agreed to take the heat off the situation by flying out to Portugal to join Louis Edwards, who was there with United's youth squad for a tournament ('The players were marvellous to me. They tried to cheer me up with shouts of "Good morning, boss, how's it going?"') but within days he could stand it no longer and was flying back to Mary's side, determined to confront the critics alongside her.

I'd gone to Portugal to get away from the publicity. We never spoke about Mary. I got the feeling that Big Louis and his board felt it was a private matter and had nothing really to do with the club as such. I got the impression that the chairman had made up his own mind that I was staying on as manager. When I flew back to Manchester I genuinely thought it had blown over. I looked forward to working normally again and made a vow to myself that I would win United the title and prove that my ability to manage the club had not been affected.

He was living in false hope.

It soon became clear through attitudes towards me
and innuendo in conversation that the 'junior board'
had been doing its stirring. These self-opinionated
and self-appointed friends of the directors and players
had been hard at it keeping the pot boiling. They had
wanted me out for a long time and were determined
not to let their opportunity go by. I wasn't too worried
about them. But I was bothered that I hadn't yet had
the chance to speak to Sir Matt Busby.

I didn't take him into my confidence over Mary
because I always knew that he was such a man of
principles that he would not have liked the situation.
For my part I believed my only crime was that,
although I was married, I had fallen in love with
another woman. But would he see it as simply as that?
He's a wonderful man and never bears grudges, and I
know he would rather say a good word about someone
than a bad one. He was always prepared to help you.
It was for all those reasons that I just didn't feel it
would be right to tell him. In fact, I don't think I
really had the courage to tell him. I was torn between
my love for her and not wanting to keep it a secret
from Sir Matt and the board. I had been going out
with Mary for nearly two years and I am convinced no
one at the club had known apart from Laurie Brown,
who actually used to baby-sit for us. If anyone did
know they certainly didn't say anything about it. If it
had been an open secret I'm sure Sir Matt would have
called me on one side and challenged me about it.

The media heat engulfing the couple was so intense
it was becoming impossible to lead a normal life. Mary
appeared to be standing up to it stoically, but they agreed
it might cool things down if Docherty went away for a

few days. He was reluctant to leave her, but she had her children to look after and couldn't easily slip away. And so, with mixed feelings, Docherty headed for the Lake District where friends owned a hotel. In the boot of his car was the FA Cup: 'I'd promised to show it to my friends at the hotel so they could have some photographs with it. It also reminded me of happier moments.'

Now the club was emphatically denying that the reason he had gone away was because he had been suspended, and Louis Edwards was again vigorously denying that he would be sacked. But one twist to the story increased Docherty's own doubts about his future. Sir Matt Busby, who had been on holiday, had returned and was reported to be 'deeply disturbed' at Docherty having set up home with Mary Brown.

Docherty spent an uneasy weekend in the Lakes – he recognised the serious view Sir Matt must by now have taken of the whole business – and was pondering what best to do next when just after breakfast on the Monday he got a telephone call. On the line was the Manchester United secretary, Les Olive, telling him icily that he must return immediately and be at Louis Edwards's home by two o'clock that afternoon for a special meeting of the board. The urgency sounded ominous.

After a tortured drive south he eased his Mercedes into the driveway leading up to the chairman's front door. He walked briskly to the house, reassuring himself that it was probably a straightforward 'clear the air' meeting, but his intuition told him that he had been called to be given a verdict on his career at Old Trafford. He knocked on the big door with mixed feelings. Mrs Edwards answered, brought him a cup of tea and asked him to wait: 'She was very kind to me.'

Fifteen minutes went by before Docherty was asked to go into the lounge. United's big six were there: chairman Edwards, Sir Matt Busby, Bill Young, Denzil Haroun and Alan Gibson and the chairman's son, Martin. The secretary Les Olive was also present. The atmosphere was solemn.

> I sat down and could see that the chairman seemed embarrassed. There was what you would call an awkward silence. I was invited to give my side of recent events. Nobody said anything about the situation which had led up to the meeting. It was obvious that they'd all had their say and now any statement would have to come from the chairman himself. I looked at Big Louis and he was clearly very uneasy about what was happening.

Louis Edwards broke the silence. 'Under the circumstances we think it would be in the best interests of everyone concerned if you resign as manager, Tommy.'

The words punched into Docherty. This was the end of the road. 'I tried to respond but could hardly get the words out. Here was my wonderful chairman and pal stamping on my life's work and for what . . . for falling in love with Mary.'

He struggled for control and told his chairman defiantly, 'Why should I resign? I haven't done anything wrong.'

If being asked to resign had stunned him, the next

statement, from Martin Edwards, left him flabbergasted: 'We believe you have been selling Cup-final tickets.'

Docherty looked at Martin incredulously. 'Of course I have. I've been selling Cup-final tickets since coming into football. I sold some of your dad's last year, and your brother's. And I sold tickets for other people at the club.'

It was Martin's turn to appear embarrassed, but he did not respond to Docherty's admission. Docherty decided it was time to do some straight talking. 'What am I here for?' he demanded to know. 'My affair with Mary Brown, or for selling Cup-final tickets? If I'm here for selling tickets then I should have been here last year and the year before.'

The directors shuffled uneasily. Docherty felt they were looking for an excuse because they did not want to say that the affair with Mary was the only reason they wanted him out. Being accused of selling tickets was a red herring.

When no response came from the directors, he fired back angrily: 'I won't resign.'

Chairman Edwards intervened again. 'Tommy, if you won't resign we'll have to sack you,' he warned.

I'd gone into the meeting prepared for the sack but living in hope that I would survive. When Big Louis said those words I knew there was no escape route. I looked across at Sir Matt. He said nothing, but I could tell he was genuinely upset it had come to this. As I drove from the chairman's house that afternoon I was close to tears. I didn't think it was necessary to throw me out of my job.

Docherty went to his Old Trafford office for the last time the next morning to collect his personal belongings and clear out his desk.

> I said cheerio to the staff and knew they were all as upset as I was. They were friendly people and it had got to them. I've no doubt the 'junior board' were delighted. But they were a contemptible bunch. They thought they had influence but they had none really. Big Louis despised them.
>
> The fans were magnificent to me. I got thousands of letters of support saying I shouldn't have been sacked. What frustrated me most of all was that my plans for the team were now in tatters. I would not be the one who would be making the decisions and that hurt. I was leaving a young side that had just won the FA Cup and I knew we could have gone on from there to more honours. The team had only one old head in it, and that was Jimmy Greenhoff. The win over Liverpool at Wembley had proved to me they could mix it with the best.

He had already hatched his plan to make the team into a title-winning side. His target was the Leicester and England goalkeeper Peter Shilton, 'the best in the business', to replace Alex Stepney who'd done 'a marvellous job' but was coming to the end of his career. The money to buy Shilton was available (£1m had already been added to the profits) and Docherty's firm view was that 'he would have given us that steel at the back which would have made us into a cracking team'. He was only waiting for the right moment to discuss it with the chairman.

Docherty would not only miss out on the chance to

buy Peter Shilton but on a bumper pay rise too: 'The chairman had promised a big rise for winning the Cup. I was earning £18,000 a year and he offered me £25,000, a small fortune then. He had also promised a bonus of £5,000 for the Cup. When we won it he told me he was giving me £15,000 instead, he was that pleased.'

There was also a new four-year contract up to 1981 that had been offered. Docherty had delayed signing because he wanted to tell the club about his involvement with Mary Brown first. 'Once they gave me the sack I knew there would be no going back on it. If they had asked me to stay it would have been tantamount to them admitting they had made a mistake in the first place. I would have dearly loved to have gone back because I felt I had done nothing wrong.'

He admits to being 'annoyed' at the manner of his departure but he stands loyally by the United banner.

I love to see them doing well. United is still my club at heart, and I would have walked back and worked for nothing if I had been given a second chance. British football *needs* a successful Manchester United. Wherever they go they attract big crowds, which is good for other clubs and the game as a whole. I think the Munich crash has added to the legend when people remember that wonderful young team being wiped out. A wave of affection from all over the world followed the club after that. New support came to the fore and has stayed loyal.

Many times Docherty has tried to analyse the day of the fateful meeting which left his career in ruins.

The bandwagon had hit the buffers, but why? He tried desperately to rationalise events. 'There had been a sudden change of heart. One day I was staying, the next I was forced out. I just could not believe that the situation could have turned against me so quickly. Something was not right.'

Informed gossip at the time speculated on a complexity of reasons for his rapid demise. Some suggested the strong Roman Catholic influence at United had made people much concerned about his personal life and that that had been the key factor; others that outraged wives had threatened to boycott the club if he stayed.

His instinct that other factors had been at work gained credence years later when a friend told him that, on the morning of the meeting at the home of Louis Edwards, two members of the Old Trafford staff had called at the house for a private chat with the chairman. They were Laurie Brown and Johnny Aston, a former United and England full-back.

> I believe that what was said at that meeting led to the sudden change of heart and my downfall. But I have no regrets. I've been very happy with Mary, and Manchester United have been trying to replace me ever since.

12 In the Courts

At the age of 49 and in the process of building a new domestic life, Tommy Docherty was out of a job, not to mention shell-shocked at being thrown out by the club he revered above all others. It was a daunting prospect, only partly relieved by an approach from the Norwegian club Lillestrom with whom he made a verbal agreement with the proviso that, if he changed his mind before the starting date, he would not be held to it.

In the event he did change his mind and the Norwegians threatened to sue, but as there was nothing in writing and they had been warned of the possibility, nothing came of it, although it was the forerunner of more earnest legal troubles to come.

The switch in direction was towards first-division Derby County. Friends had often played a part in helping to rescue his career when things had gone wrong, and this time it was Tom Pendry, Labour MP for Stalybridge, who lived near Docherty in Charlesworth.

Pendry was a keen Derby supporter and he arranged for me to meet the Derby chairman, George Hardy. We clinched my appointment as manager there and then, a contract and terms. It was a new challenge. It suited me and I lived a short drive from the Baseball Ground. Everything seemed right – especially when George Hardy told me I would be the first manager in the Football League to run a Rolls-Royce. The trouble was, he had no money to spend. It was a question of selling a player to buy one.

Docherty quickly found a familiar situation at Derby: just as there had been at Aston Villa and at Manchester United, there were cliques to contend with.

Another complication was that the club had a strict rule that no player could be sold to Nottingham Forest. The ghost of Brian Clough still walked the corridors at the Baseball Ground where he'd had so much success. The Derby directors clearly couldn't stand Clough's success at Forest after he had left them. He wanted to buy Charlie George from us . . . I agreed . . . the board blocked the sale. That's how small-minded it had become. I was told Brian never went to Derby board meetings. I'm not surprised. You could never get much sense out of the directors there. One director was a self-appointed boardroom spy who used to go round the club checking up on people to see if they were enjoying extras.

I liked George Hardy but he just wasn't strong enough for the job. He talked a good game but had never played it and eventually he was pushed out. An accountant took over, Mr Moore. I told him he knew the price of everything and the value of nothing. No wonder Cloughie couldn't stand them.

On one occasion Derby and QPR were both struggling against relegation. It came to the crunch when Rangers had to go to Leeds where defeat would send them down. Five of the six Derby directors went to Elland

Road and left us at the Baseball Ground. I called
them the crazy gang.

Curiously enough, Rangers' losing was to affect his
career at Derby. On being relegated Jim Gregory asked
him back again to Shepherd's Bush: 'Derby wanted a
yes-man and I was too strong for that. I think they were
glad to see me go to Rangers . . . but would Jim want a
yes-man? It would be interesting.'

Just over ten years had elapsed since his dramatic
walk-out on Queen's Park Rangers when he began a
second spell as manager of the London club, in May
1979. Chairman Jim Gregory persuaded him that this
time it would be different and he agreed they must have
both learned from their earlier disastrous experience.

He noticed from the start that the club had a flourishing
youth policy. When the season opened in August 1979
he immediately gave youth its chance, bringing in Paul
Goddard and Clive Allen, a young lad who would go on to
become one of the country's most prolific goal-scorers at
other London clubs and in France. His first few months in
charge were encouraging, with Rangers well placed near
the top of the second division, but an ugly incident with
hooligans was to cost him and the team dearly. The team
had drawn at home with Wrexham and he was travelling
from London to the home he still had on the outskirts
of Manchester when the trouble engulfed him.

On the journey a bunch of youths started singing
abusive songs about him and Mary Brown. He confronted
them, asking them to behave, and the incident seemed to

pass until he was leaving the train at Stockport. As he opened the carriage door he was attacked by the same youths who knocked him to the ground and kicked him about the head and body before running off. An ambulance was called and police arrived on the scene. Battered and bruised, the semi-conscious Docherty was given oxygen on the platform and rushed to hospital where it was found he had suffered ruptured tendons in his knee. His leg was put in plaster and he was detained for a week before being allowed home where he was to spend another five weeks recovering. By that time his team, without its manager, had hit a losing run taking just 2 points from six games and slipping out of the promotion race. Still, he managed to pull things round and results improved when he returned from his injuries but the damage had already been done and Rangers finished 4 points short of a promotion place.

He was promptly sacked in a piece of pure theatre that was to enliven many of his after-dinner speeches in the years ahead. Jim Gregory called him into the office and told him it was the parting of their ways. Docherty responded warmly: 'Don't go, chairman, I think you are doing a good job.' Gregory saw the funny side but quickly informed him that he was the one who was leaving.

The players pleaded on his behalf and he was immediately reinstated, but they couldn't save him when Jim Gregory sacked him a second time early the following season. The chain of events leading to his final dismissal began when he agreed to sign Andy Ritchie from his former club, Manchester United.

I had taken Andy to United when I was manager there and knew he was a good player. Jim Gregory did the groundwork brilliantly in setting up the deal for me to bring him to Rangers.

It went sour, however, when the United manager, Dave Sexton, who had replaced Docherty at Old Trafford, had second thoughts. Docherty was furious and tactlessly said so in the press. He went further when told that first division Brighton had agreed to buy Ritchie and that his former club Chelsea, now back in the second division, were also showing an interest. Docherty said publicly again that Ritchie was a first-division player and should be going to a first-division club.

Chelsea responded furiously to what they believed was his unnecessary interference. His remarks had been interpreted in the press as being advice to Ritchie not to join Chelsea and, unsurprisingly, they complained bitterly to Jim Gregory, who was also irritated by his manager's public comments; an apology was offered to Chelsea. Andy Ritchie did in fact join Brighton but the events had undermined Docherty's position and he was again sacked by Rangers for his indiscretions in October 1980.

This was serious, for he had a perjury case and possible jail hanging over him, and he recognised other English clubs would be unwilling to offer him a job until the trial was out of the way. However, a friend from his playing days had recommended him to the Australian club Sydney Olympic, who were looking for a part-time coach, and he accepted the job. 'It was a good offer, the money was good and it gave me the chance to stay working with players.' The standard was similar to the lower divisions of the Football League, with matches played on Sundays. He knew, though, that it was a short-term job and eight months later, in June 1981 when his contract was finished, he returned to England where Preston North End had offered him the manager's job although the perjury trial was now only four months away.

In the four years up to the autumn of 1981 Docherty endured personal discomfort and psychological pressures on a scale that would have broken the spirit of a lesser man. The traumatic events unfolded between 4 July 1977, when he was ignominiously sacked as manager of Manchester United, and 20 October 1981, the day he was cleared by an Old Bailey jury on two counts of perjury which lifted the threat of him going to prison.

The perjury trial had arisen from a High Court libel action he impulsively embroiled himself in which went disastrously wrong. As if that wasn't enough, while he was coming to terms with the humiliating and costly effects of the libel case, he was arrested over alleged irregularities concerning the transfer of players while he was manager at Derby County.

Docherty came through it all not unscathed but with typical mischievous humour: 'I've been in more courts than Bjorn Borg,' he said when asked about his legal problems. The humour merely masked the seriousness of the events which had inevitably left their mark on him both emotionally and financially.

His problems had begun early in 1977, while he was still manager of Manchester United, when one of his former players Willie Morgan criticised him on a Granada television programme. Morgan had said that he was 'about the worst manager' he had ever played under. Legal advisers told him that he could launch a successful libel action against the player and television company, and he decided to go ahead. He was in fact acting against his own instincts which had always been to give criticism and take it without reacting.

By the time the libel action reached the High Court in November 1978, he was managing Derby County. On the opening day of the case the High Court heard that Willie Morgan had been made captain of Manchester United by Docherty and was one of the stars of the team, playing at his peak. But in the summer of 1974 Morgan had suffered a serious eye injury while playing tennis and it had affected his football, Docherty's counsel told the court. Morgan asked for a transfer and went to Burnley for £30,000 before eventually moving on to Bolton Wanderers. Counsel for Docherty said Morgan had left Manchester United with a deep-seated grudge. Docherty told the High Court he had been 'very upset' at Morgan's remarks on television about him being such a bad manager, and rejected also further comments from Morgan that there would be rejoicing in Manchester when he left the club.

On the third day of the High Court action Docherty dropped the libel action and withdrew all allegations against Willie Morgan and Granada TV after admitting under cross-examination that he had told lies over the 'free' transfer of former Scottish international Denis Law from United.

After dropping the case Docherty was left with a bill for legal costs estimated at over £30,000, but an incalculable cost in lost opportunities and loss of face was the inevitable consequence. And though the High Court was behind him the Old Bailey awaited, where he would have to answer for 'lying on oath' during the libel action.

Of the case, Docherty says now,

> There was a tremendous sense of relief when Willie Morgan's eye operation was successful, although we were warned that he might have problems with his sight. It was obvious Willie would miss the pre-season training while he recovered but we all hoped very much that he would be as good as ever, because he was a superb player.

Morgan, a naturally fit player, trained hard and played in over thirty first-team games the following season of 1974–75, but Docherty judged he was not the player he had been before his injury. 'I just wondered if he was seeing the ball as clearly since he'd had his eye operation.' Meanwhile Docherty had moved to sign Steve Coppell from Tranmere Rovers. He felt Coppell had the quality and pace eventually to replace Morgan, although his original intention had been that Morgan would remain at his peak for another couple of seasons.

Coppell, who was to play with distinction for United and England, began his Old Trafford career in cracking form and Docherty decided to give him his chance in the first team.

> Willie's form was patchy, but when I left him out
> of the team he always took it badly. When he was
> substitute he wouldn't join his team-mates for the
> warm-up before a game and became very sulky. I
> wanted him to stay because he was still a fine player
> and I liked him. But Willie wouldn't listen. He was
> popular with the fans and was heading for a bumper
> testimonial payday which was only a couple of seasons
> away.

In April 1979, five months after the libel case, Docherty resigned as manager of Derby County and the following month started his second spell at Queen's Park Rangers. His problems continued with a vengeance. In bed at the Kensington Hilton Hotel one morning he answered a knock on the door, to be confronted by two policemen from the Derby force. He was arrested and taken to Derby by car immediately to face a police grilling into alleged irregularities over players going to America while he was manager at Derby County. Asked why he had given one player a free transfer and yet a year later the same player was bought by another club for £30,000, an exasperated Docherty explained that it was normal football practice. He had been pruning his staff at the Baseball Ground and felt he had better players than the one to whom he had given the free transfer. He also reminded the police during his ten-hour interrogation that the club directors were also involved in transfer discussions, not just the manager, and he had made nothing out of the deal personally. Docherty was released and the issue came to nothing, although he again had to dig deep into his pocket to meet a £3,000 legal bill.

Four months after arriving back from Sydney Olympic he was facing the biggest test of his life when his perjury trial opened at the Old Bailey with the possibility of going to jail. During the week-long hearing he was accused of deliberately lying during the High Court libel action.

Two counts against him alleged that he falsely swore on oath during the High Court proceedings that when he spoke to former Manchester United player Denis Law about a 'free' transfer Law had not seemed 'disturbed or surprised'. He had also said he did not know of a term in an agreement relating to the transfer of striker Ted McDougall under which United would pay Bournemouth a further £25,000 when McDougall had scored twenty goals . . . until United were sued.

Docherty insisted at the trial that he had not deliberately lied but had become 'hopelessly confused' by the high pressure of the cross-examination he had undergone. Richard du Cann, QC, defending him, told the jury he had been 'psychologically crippled' during the libel proceedings where he had found the witness box the 'loneliest place in the world'. Despite his years in the game dealing with press conferences and television interviews Docherty had been 'bamboozled' in the High Court.

The jury acquitted him on both counts by unanimous verdicts after a two-hour retirement. At last his ordeal was over.

In the summer of 1981 Docherty's career was to complete a thirty-two-year circle when he was invited back to struggling Preston North End to renew his friendship with Tom Finney, now the club president. Chairman Alan Jones paid £30,000 compensation to Sydney Olympic, and Docherty was received like a pop star by the public.

> It was like coming home. Preston was my first English club when I left Scotland and I still had many friends in the town. It was a joy to be back and to chat about old times with Tom Finney.

One of his first impulses was to go into the dressing-room at Deepdale.

> It brought memories flooding back. I sat by the very peg where I had hung my clothes when changing into my Preston North End shirt for the first time all those years before in 1949. They called the club Proud Preston, and I felt proud to be back amongst those wonderful people.

Docherty was to suffer more heartache. He had completed his first major deal for Preston when the bombshell dropped and his Preston honeymoon was over, after just five months.

> I sold the centre-half Bill Baxter to Middlesbrough for £400,000. I was thinking I'd done a good deal, having made the club a small fortune by selling Baxter, when the chairman called me in and said the team's results were not good enough and gave me the sack. I told him he wanted success in forty-eight hours, and

as a parting shot told him he should have left me in Australia.

In June 1984, after two more spells coaching in Australia, where he had made many friends in 1980, Docherty was back in full-time management at Wolverhampton Wanderers. The club had just dropped into the second division, and manager Graham Hawkins had paid the price with his job at the end of April. Wolves were in a desperate position, struggling to cope with falling attendances and rising debts, and they needed a boost to their flagging morale. A disgruntled supporter summed up the mood surrounding the once-proud club when he wrote a letter to the new incumbent telling him he was a 'lucky man' because he hadn't seen the team in action the previous season. It amused Docherty, and he wisecracked at his first press conference after taking charge that, whereas he had 'shopped at Harrods' during the golden days at Chelsea, now 'I'll be going to the nearest cash and carry'.

The prevailing mood at the club severely restricted Docherty's natural management style and wheeler-dealing, and made it virtually impossible for him to rebuild a playing staff already demoralised by relegation. Three months into his first season, with results continuing to disappoint, his assistant Jim Barron was fired. Christmas brought little cheer, and speculation was increasing that an overseas consortium was planning a £4 million take-over package for the club. Uncertainty about the future off the pitch was reflected in dismal performances on it, and the team slipped towards relegation yet again. In May 1985 they slumped to a 1–5 defeat at Brighton which effectively condemned them to the third division for the first time in over sixty years.

Docherty's hands were tied because of the club's financial situation, and he saw relegation as the result of fifteen years of neglect. On 4 July, the eighth anniversary of his sacking by Manchester United, he was out of work again as Wolves headed for bankruptcy. His reaction: 'I felt I had finally got management out of my system.'

Nevertheless, his love of a challenge lured him back once more in 1987, although this time it was to the less stressful environment of non-League Altrincham, in leafy Cheshire, on the outskirts of Manchester. Gerry Burman, then chairman of the club, was ambitious for League football, and wanted Docherty's name and expertise to lead the campaign. 'It was a mistake,' insists Docherty. 'Gerry was a smashing chairman and a good man to work for, but there was a lot of back-stabbing at the club at that time, and it just didn't work out.'

In February 1988 a new chairman, Geoff Lloyd, took over, but by that time Docherty had decided it was time to go. The two men met to discuss the future. 'He told me the routines would not be the same under him. He pointed to a clash of personalities between us, but I said I didn't agree. I told him he had no personality, so I did not see how I could clash with him.' The two men agreed to differ, and Docherty's managerial come-back was over.

13 Docherty Speaking

For those who have watched Tommy Docherty from a distance, the picture is inevitably flawed. Stories of his sackings, scandals, court cases and brushes with authority have painted an incomplete portrait of the man who mocks his detractors by claiming to have had more clubs than Jack Nicklaus. Any judgement of Docherty demands a more personal knowledge of the man behind the headlines.

His lifelong friend, Tom Finney, welcomed Docherty back to Preston as manager in 1981 with the friendly observation that he was 'never at a loss for words'. When the music stopped on Docherty's managerial career it was the words, the wisecracks, the masterful one-liners that immediately fashioned a new direction for him as an after-dinner speaker in constant demand.

The jokes, of course, had followed him from school to be perfected as a defensive and disarming weapon throughout his career. During his perjury trial in 1981, and faced with the prospect of going to jail, he remarked to a reporter that if he was found guilty and sent down he would run the prison football team. If results went against him, he reasoned, the prison bosses would have to sack him or, if he quit, let him out.

The same wisecracking Docherty commented months later when Preston sacked him: 'It was one of the nicest sackings I have ever had.' Occasionally, though, the joke was on him. While he was coaching in Australia, one English manager observed, 'He's gone two hundred years too late.'

Docherty's more serious side could also illuminate his generosity of spirit. Dejected after his Manchester United team had been beaten by second-division Southampton in the 1976 FA Cup final, he still found time to telephone the Saints manager, Lawrie McMenemy, to tell him, 'Well done. Enjoy yourselves.'

Docherty may have finished with management, but many leading football managers are testimony to his influence. Three of his former players went on to dominate the London scene. George Graham, who played under him at Chelsea in the 1960s and became his first signing at Manchester United in the 1970s, went into management himself at Arsenal where his team won the first-division Championship twice early in his reign. Terry Venables, his argumentative young skipper at Chelsea, had a long and successful management career in Spain before taking over Spurs as manager and then managing director. In South London in the 1980s Steve Coppell, another Docherty player, was coaxing Crystal Palace into one of the first division's most improved teams.

He leaves a worthy legacy.

Docherty and Mary Brown were married in May 1988. Hundreds of guests, including personalities from the world of sport and entertainment, filled the huge marquee of their Charlesworth home, high in the Derbyshire Peaks. They have a family of their own now, daughters Grace and Lucy.

Sipping his favourite champagne, drawing contentedly on a large cigar as he looks into the flames of the open log fire – the boy from the Glasgow slums relishing his hard-earned good life – Docherty will these days readily acknowledge that life has been good to them. Looking back to the early days, the start of their relationship, he says, 'Talking to her gave me a tremendous sense of relief from the pressures of my job. She was great fun to be with. She made me feel good . . . she still does.

'We have no regrets. I still believe what happened to me at Manchester United was unnecessary, though. I wouldn't be sacked for falling in love nowadays.'

His love for the game burns as fiercely as ever. Still a regular visitor to Old Trafford as a radio commentator, he watches football as passionately from the press box as he did from the dugout. He has also tapped the deep reservoir of his experience as manager and player to build a lucrative new career on the after-dinner speaking circuit. His reputation – good and bad, fact and fiction – has gone before him with a constant stream of invitations asking him to speak at functions not only throughout Britain and the Republic of Ireland, the Middle East, Australia, even Iceland.

It is a punishing schedule. But time takes its toll, and today Docherty says: 'I might take it a little easier in future on the after-dinner circuit. I'm thinking of cutting down on my engagements to six a week.'